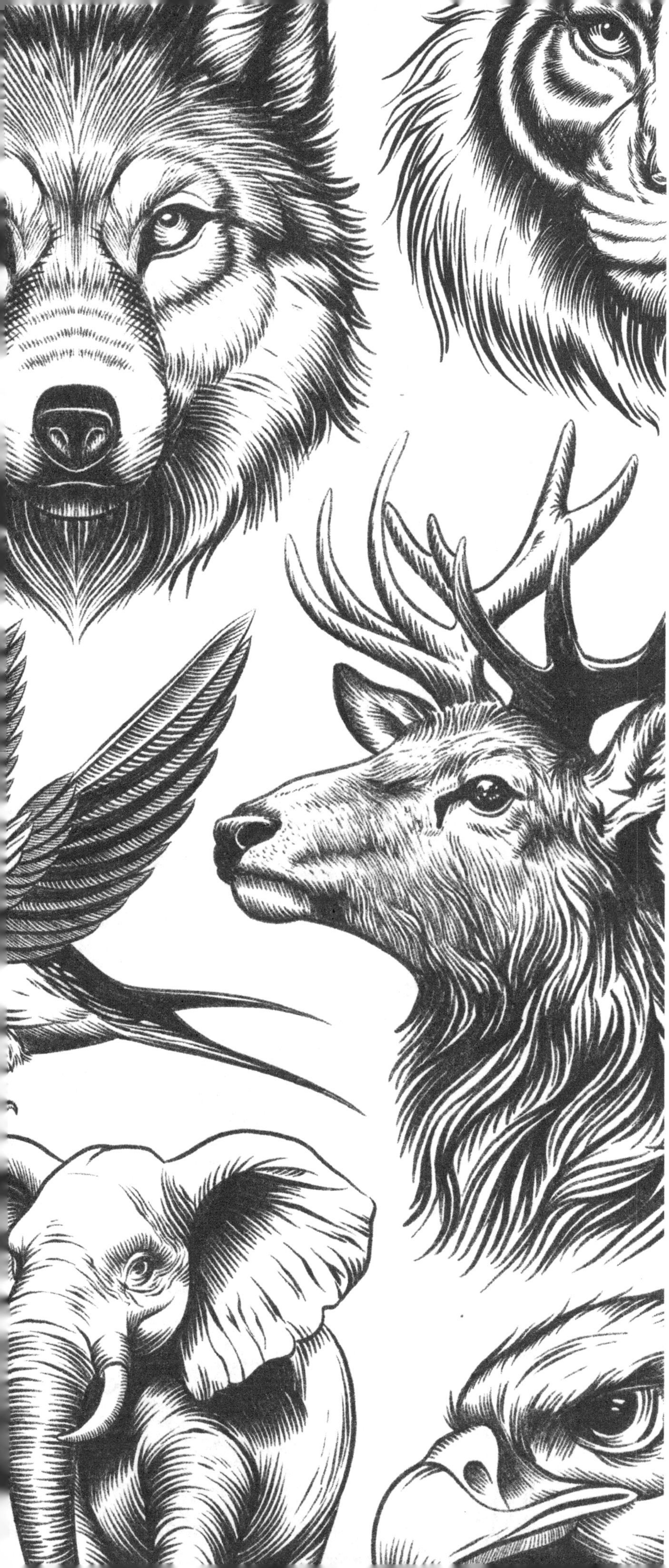

THE ART OF
DRAWING

HOW TO DRAW ANIMALS

A HELPFUL MANUAL FOR
ARTISTS AND DESIGNERS

STEP BY STEP

HAND DRAWN
UNIQUE **40** DESIGNS
BEST QUALITY

EDITIONS
Vault

INTRODUCTION

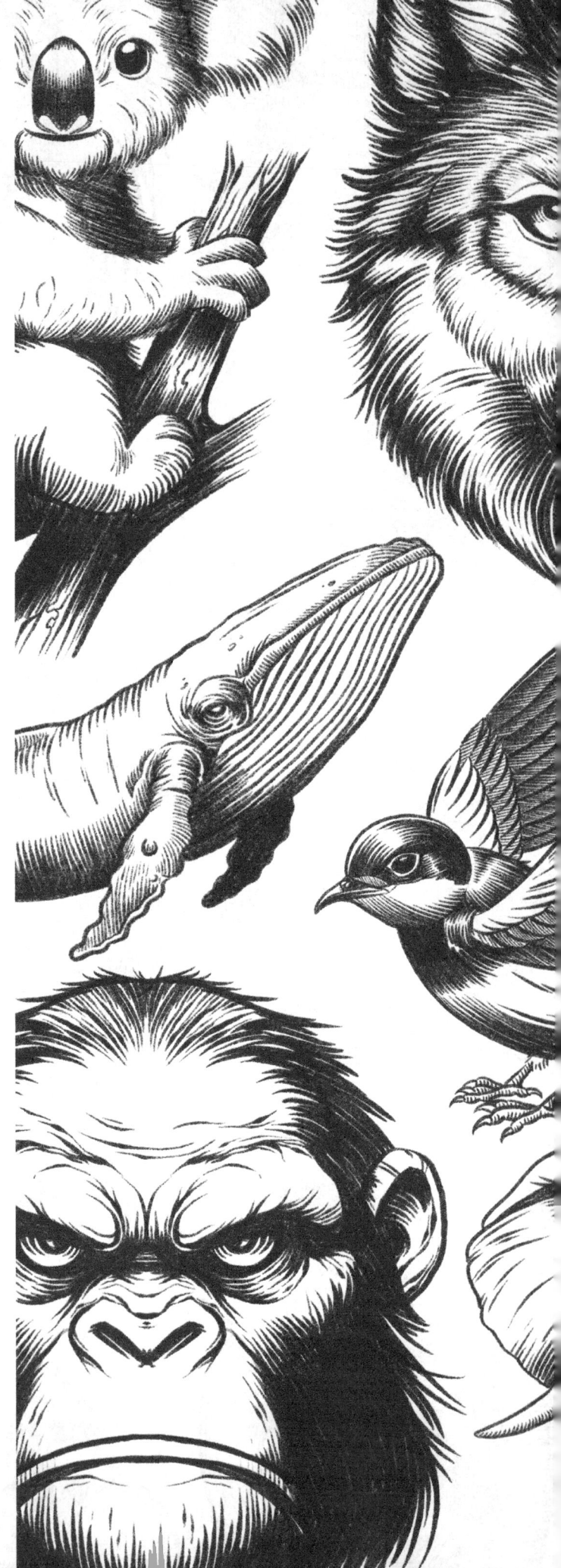

Welcome to *How to Draw Animals*, your essential guide to unlocking the secrets of drawing some of Earth's most majestic and fascinating creatures. Whether you're an aspiring artist or hobbyist or love animals and want to capture their beauty on paper, this book is designed for you.

Drawing animals can be a rewarding and inspiring experience, but it can also seem daunting if you're just starting. That's why we've created this comprehensive guide with beginners in mind, offering a progressive learning system that breaks down complex forms into manageable steps. We aim to make the process of drawing enjoyable and accessible, giving you the confidence to draw skillfully and creatively.

In the following pages, we will take you on a journey through the animal kingdom. You'll learn to draw a diverse array of animals, from the powerful and regal lion to the playful and agile dolphin. By the end of this book, you'll have developed a comprehensive set of skills, including mastery of animal anatomy, improved line work, and refined shading techniques. Your portfolio will showcase your growth and dedication as an artist, reflecting your newfound ability to confidently draw any animal with precision and creativity.

Grab your pencils, tablets, or whatever medium you prefer, and let's embark on this creative adventure together. Whether you dream of illustrating wildlife, designing captivating characters, or simply enjoying the process of drawing animals, How to Draw Animals is here to guide you every step of the way. Unleash your inner artist and bring the wonders of the animal world to life on your canvas.

vaulteditions.com

TABLE OF CONTENTS

How to Draw an Ape	01-02
How to Draw a Panther	03-04
How to Draw a Wolf	05-06
How to Draw a Polar Bear	07-08
How to Draw a Rabbit	09-10
How to Draw a Lion	11-12
How to Draw a Bat	13-14
How to Draw a Bison	15-16
How to Draw a Bear	17-18
How to Draw a Beaver	19-20
How to Draw a Butterfly	21-22
How to Draw a Cat	23-24
How to Draw a Dog	25-26
How to Draw a Dog (Doberman)	27-28
How to Draw a Shark	29-30
How to Draw a Dolphin	31-32
How to Draw a Dragonfly	33-34
How to Draw an Eagle	35-36
How to Draw an Elephant	37-38
How to Draw a Fox	39-40
How to Draw a Frog	41-42
How to Draw a Giraffe	43-44
How to Draw a Horse	45-46
How to Draw a Horse	47-48
How to Draw a Kangaroo	49-50
How to Draw a Koala	51-52
How to Draw a Lizard	53-54
How to Draw a Llama	55-56
How to Draw an Octopus	57-58
How to Draw an Owl	59-60
How to Draw a Panda	61-62
How to Draw a Penguin	63-64
How to Draw a Snake	65-66
How to Draw a Stag	67-68
How to Draw a Swallow	69-70
How to Draw a Tiger	71-72
How to Draw a Tiger	73-74
How to Draw a Walrus	75-76
How to Draw a Whale	77-78
How to Draw a Zebra	79-80

DOWNLOAD YOUR FILES

Downloading your files is simple. To access your digital files, please go to the last page of this book and follow the instructions.

For technical assistance, please email:
info@vaulteditions.com

Copyright
Copyright © Vault Editions Ltd 2023.

Bibliographical Note

This book is a new work created by Vault Editions Ltd.

ISBN: 978-1-922966-41-4

1   **VOLUME.1**   **A STEP-BY-STEP GUIDE**

APE

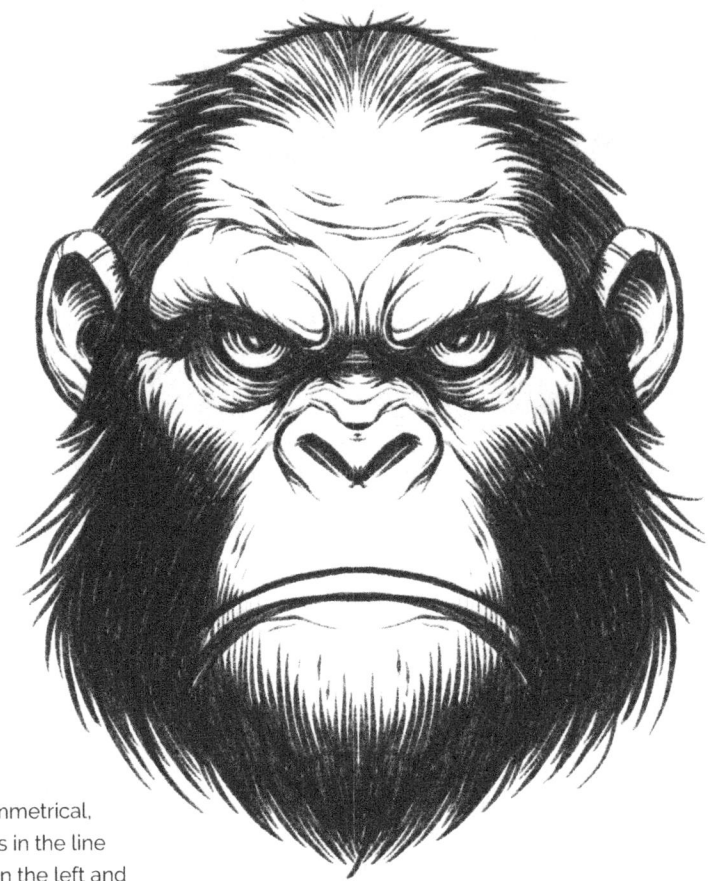

Pro Tip:
The design of the ape is symmetrical, and creating slight variations in the line work and rendering between the left and right sides of the face provides a more natural appearance.

01

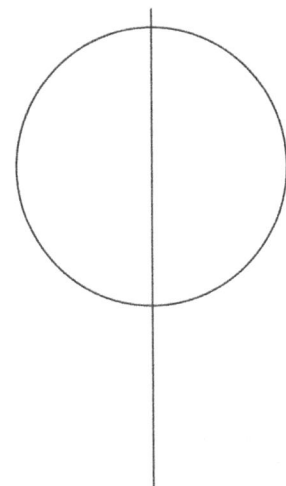

02

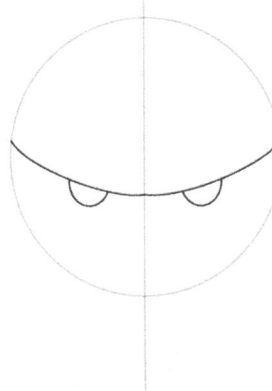

03

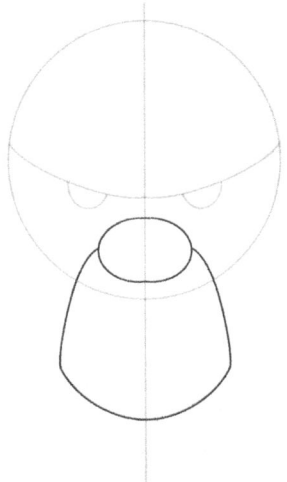

VAULTEDITIONS.COM

VOLUME.1　　　　　　　　　　　　　　　　　　　　　　　A STEP-BY-STEP GUIDE

04
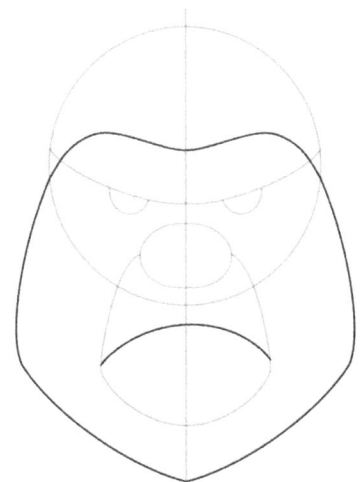

05
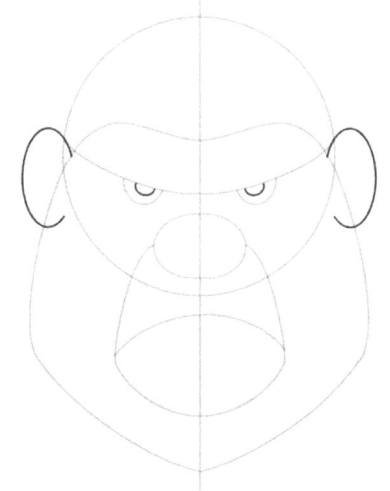

06
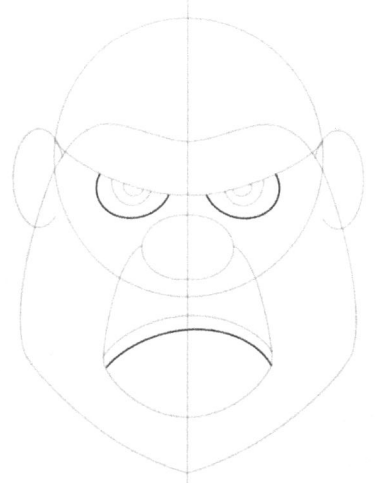

07

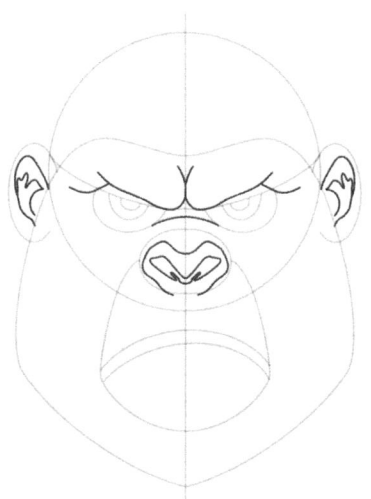

08

09
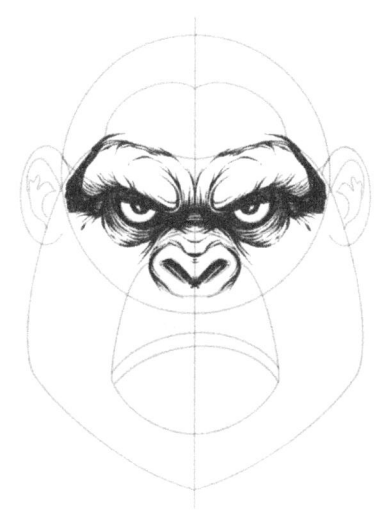

10
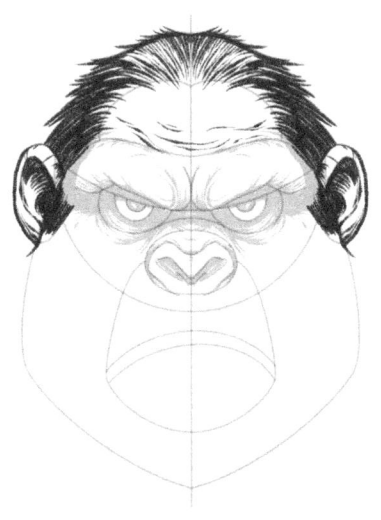

11
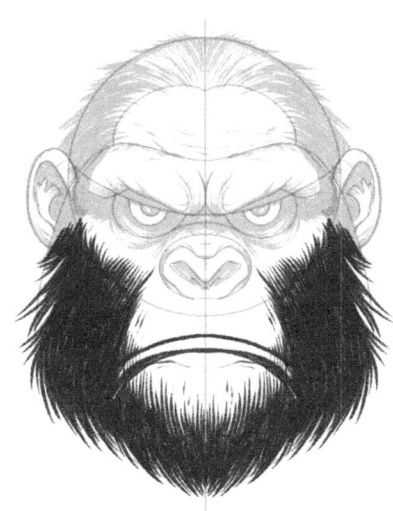

12
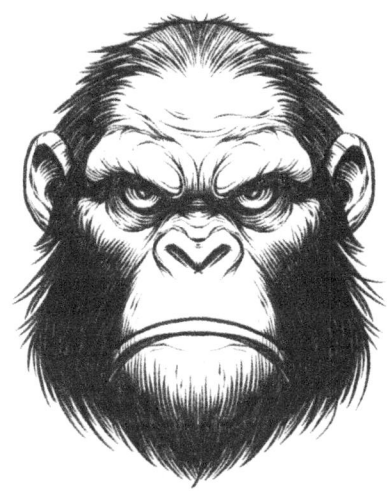

HOW TO DRAW ANIMALS

VAULTEDITIONS.COM

PANTHER

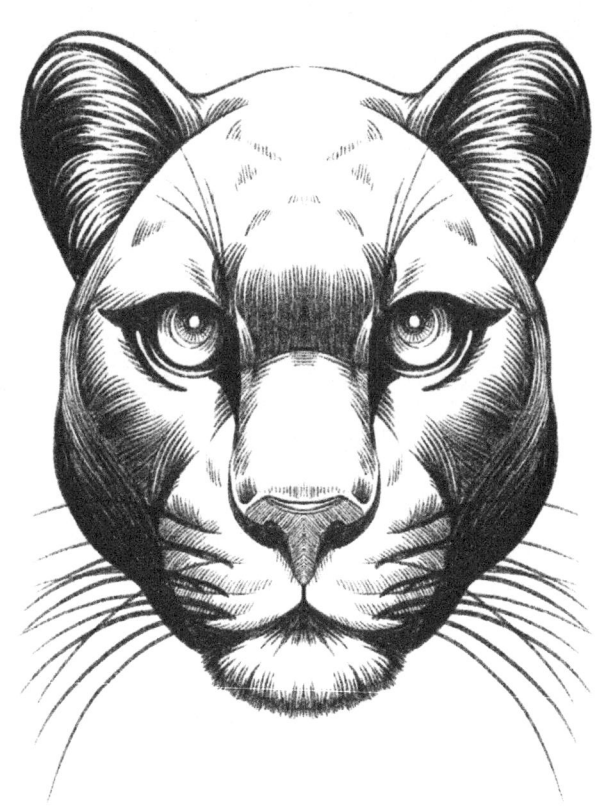

Pro Tip:
To ensure the shape of the panther's face looks natural in its proportions, draw the initial circle (the guide in step 01) slightly compressed on the vertical axis.

01

02

03

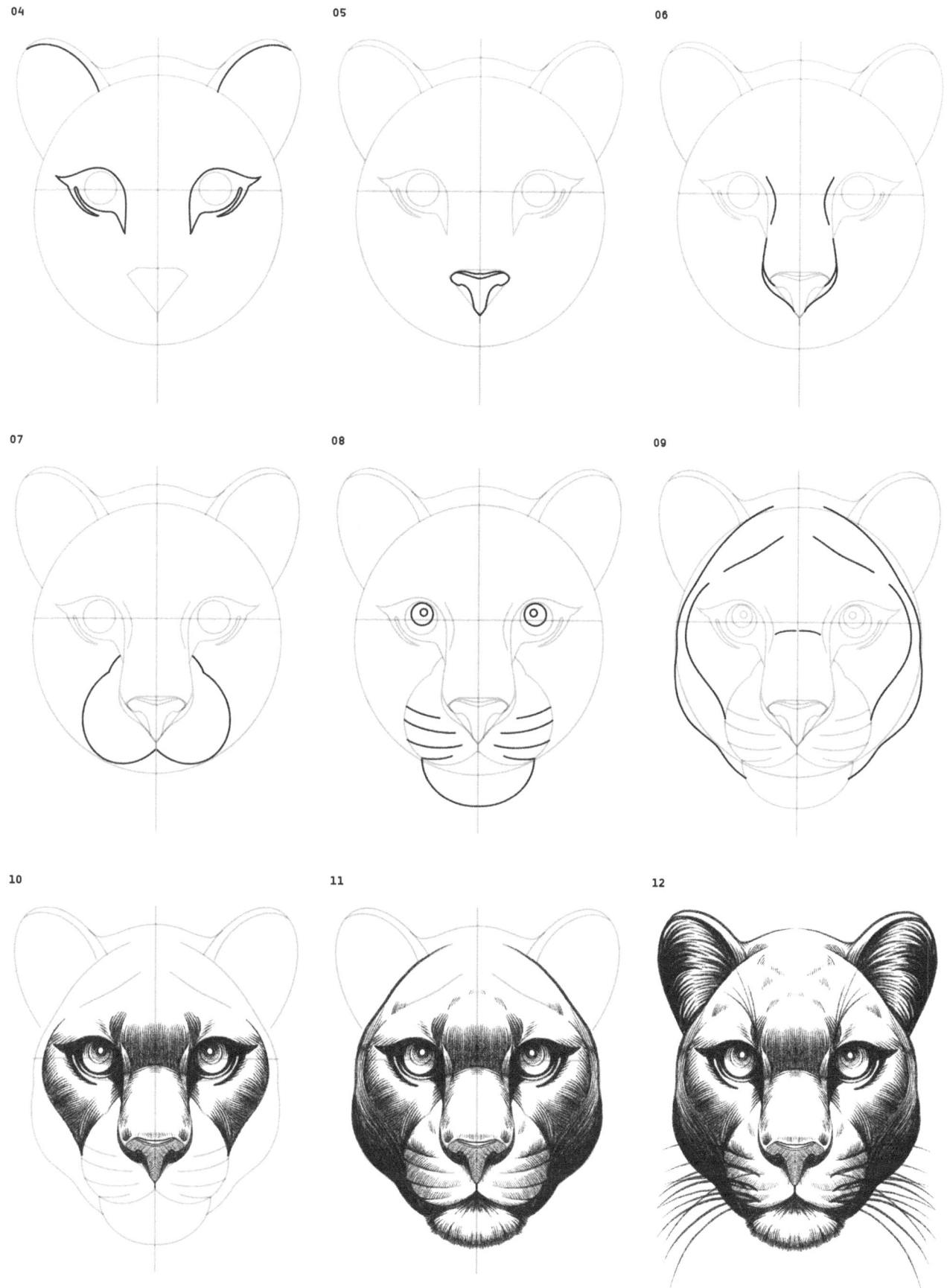

WOLF

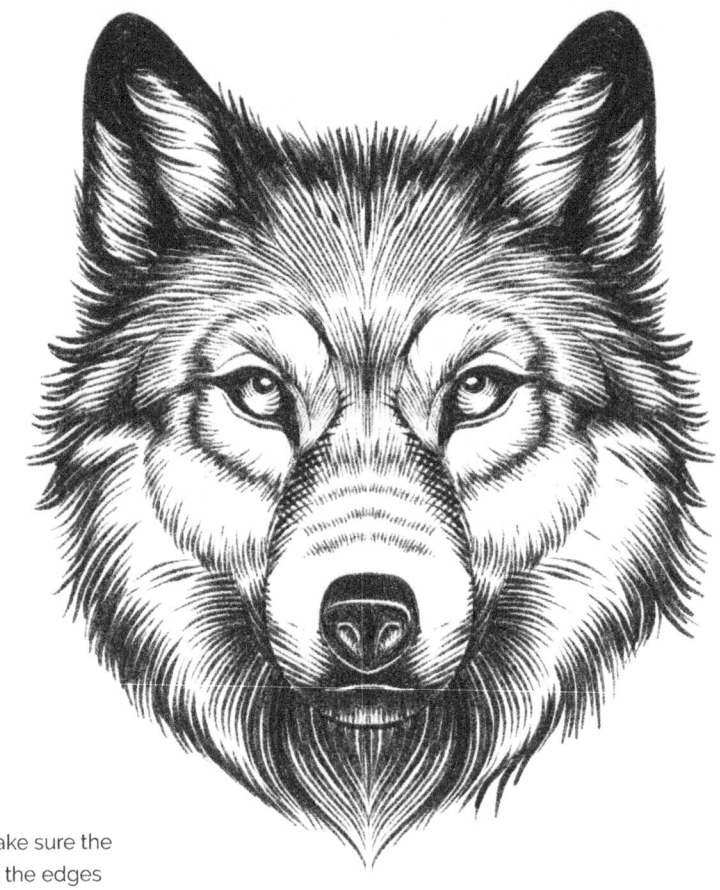

Pro Tip:
When drawing the wolf, make sure the ears are set in slightly from the edges of the head on both sides. This will help develop a more natural appearance.

01 02 03

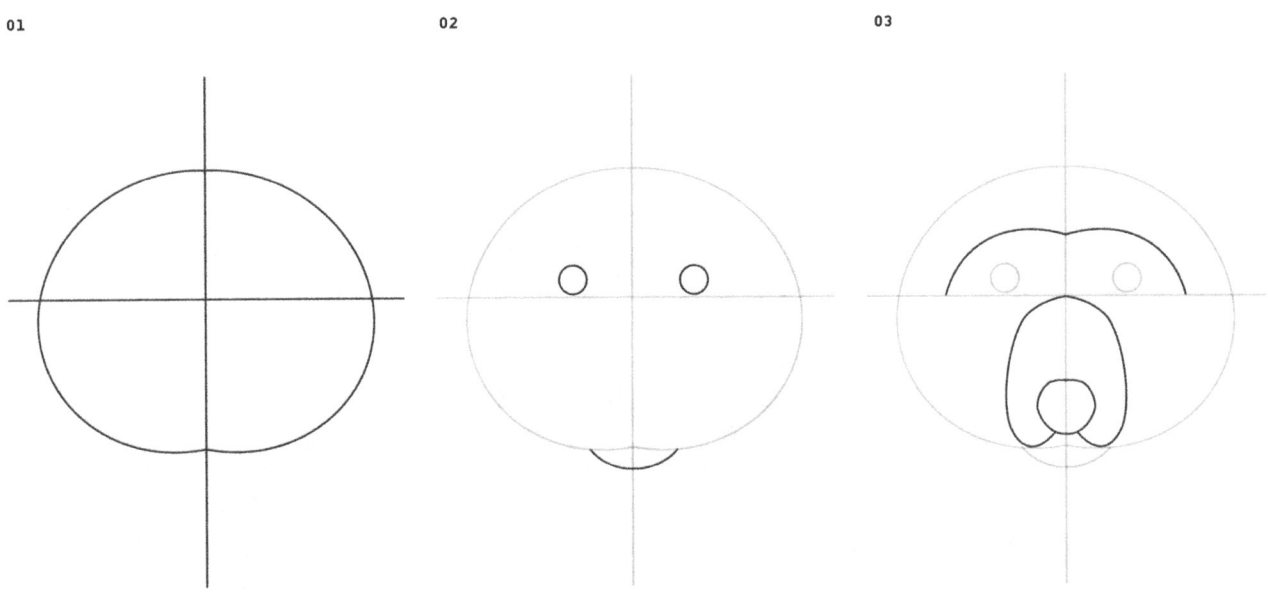

VOLUME.1 A STEP-BY-STEP GUIDE

04
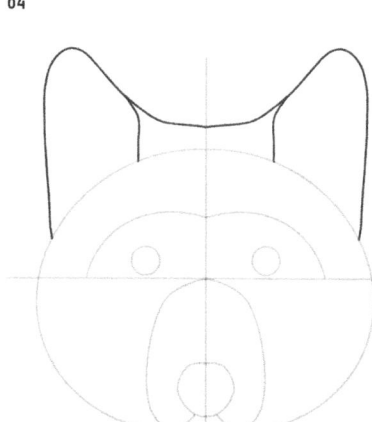

05
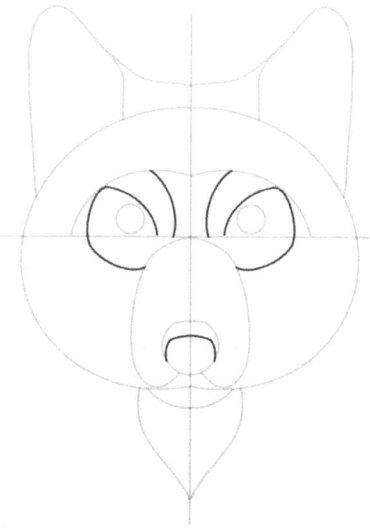

06
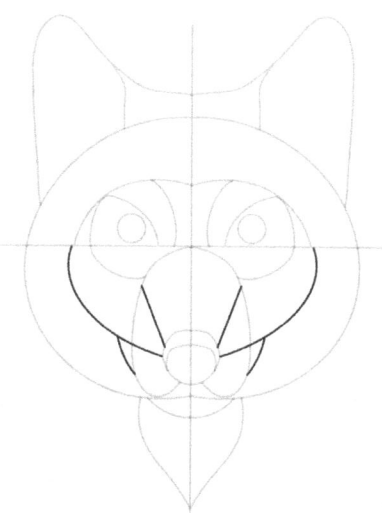

07
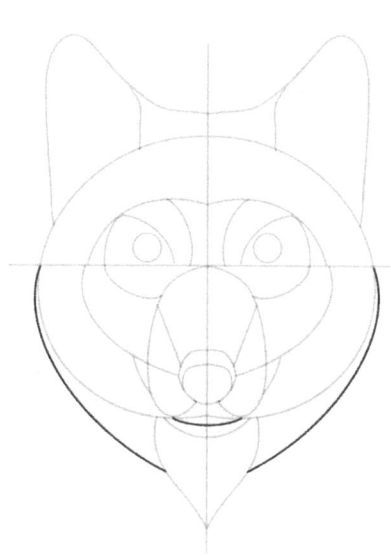

08
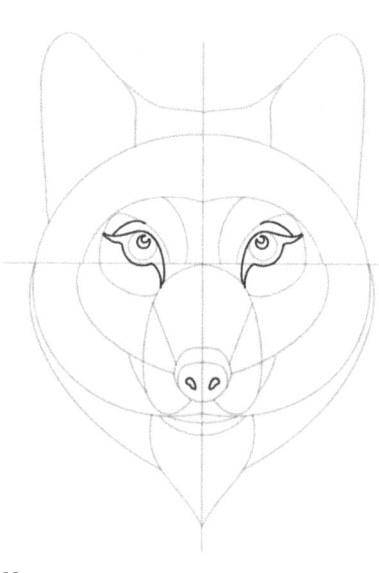

09
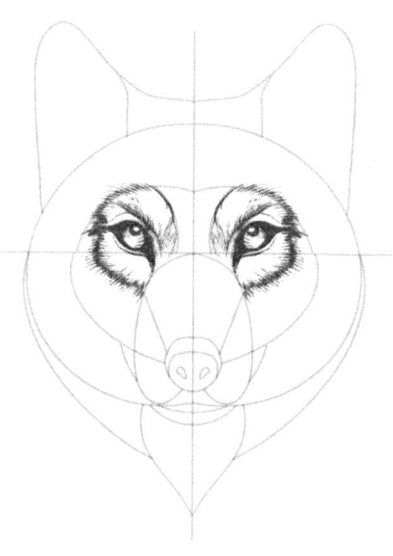

10
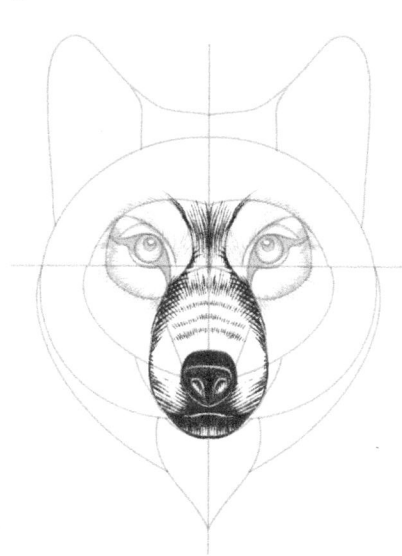

11
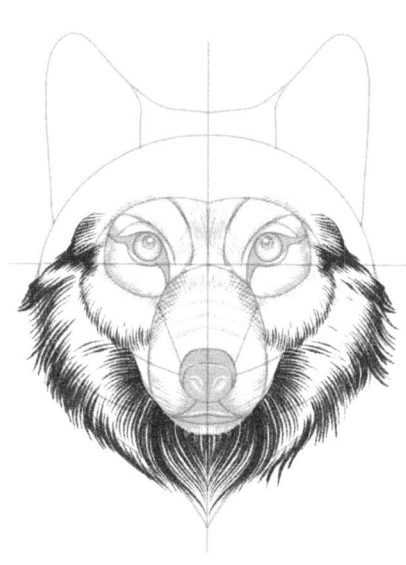

12
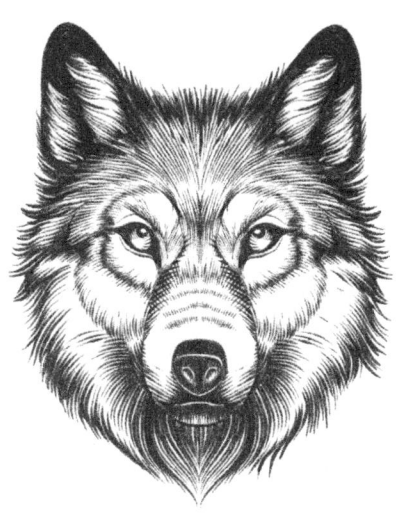

HOW TO DRAW ANIMALS

VAULTEDITIONS.COM

POLAR BEAR

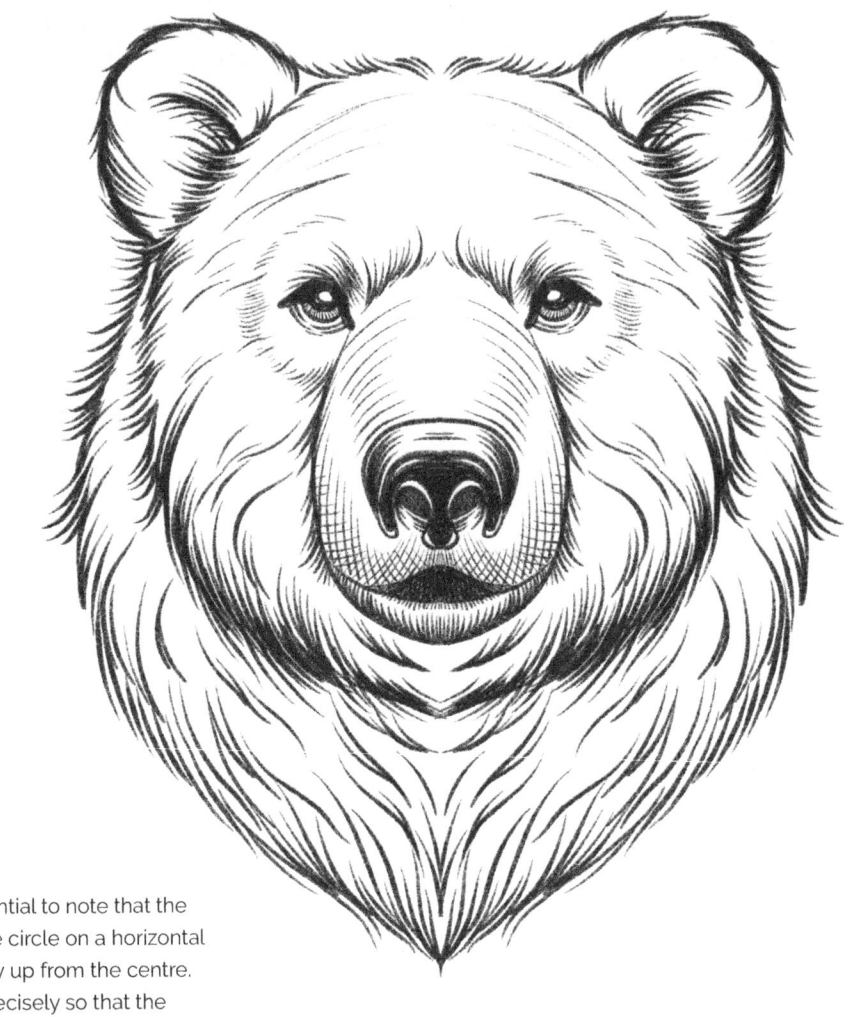

Pro Tip:
In step 01, it is essential to note that the line intersecting the circle on a horizontal axis does so slightly up from the centre. Repeat this step precisely so that the bear's face is proportioned correctly.

01 02 03

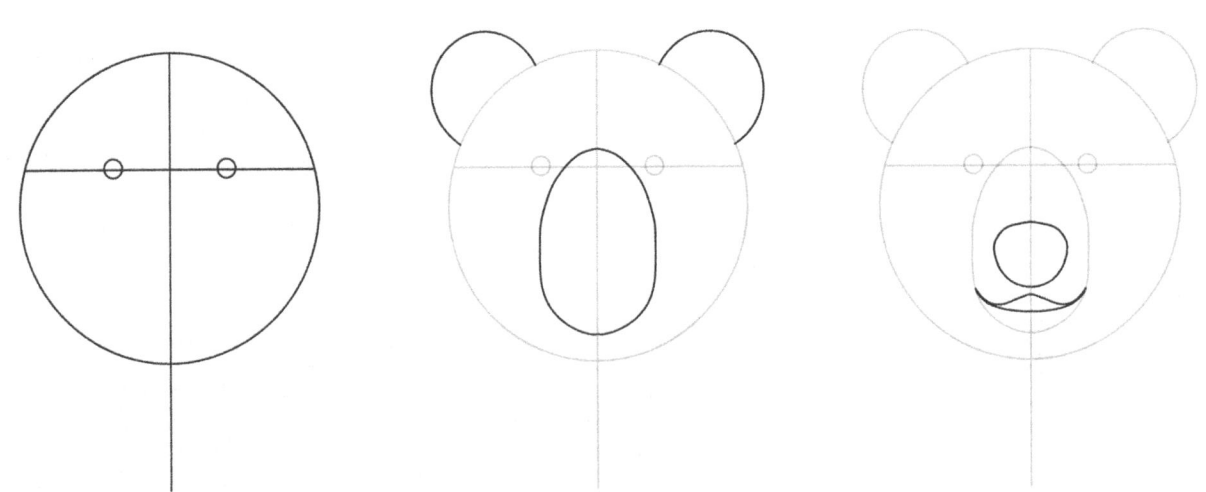

VOLUME.1 A STEP-BY-STEP GUIDE

04

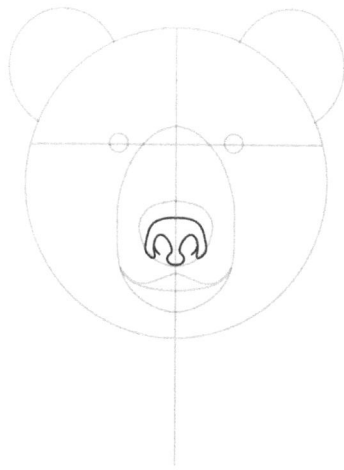

05

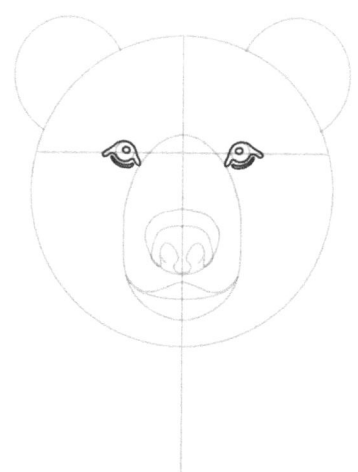

06

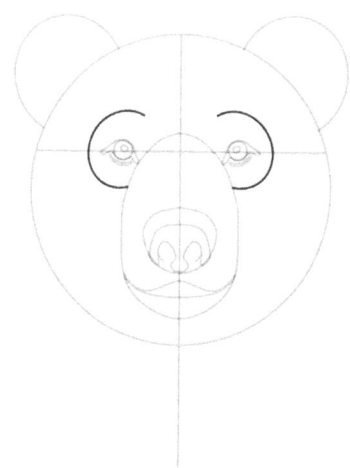

07

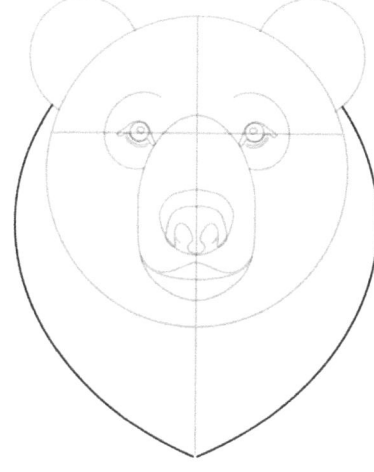

08

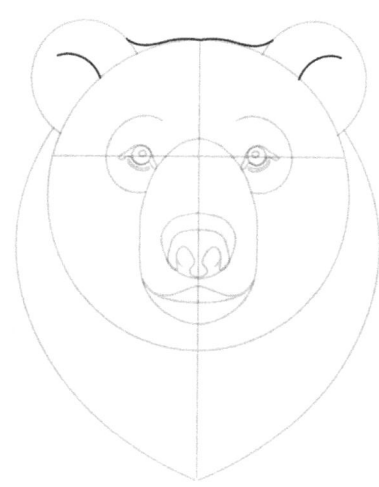

09

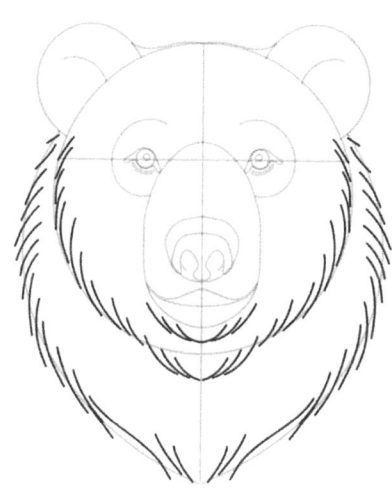

10

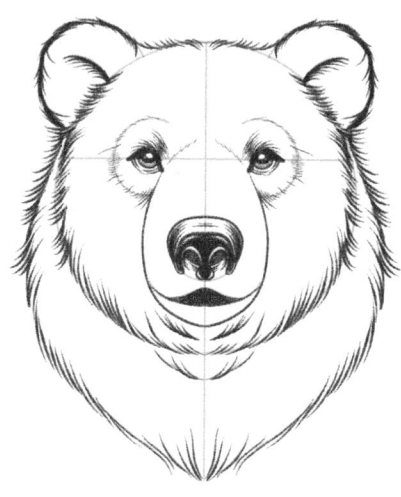

11

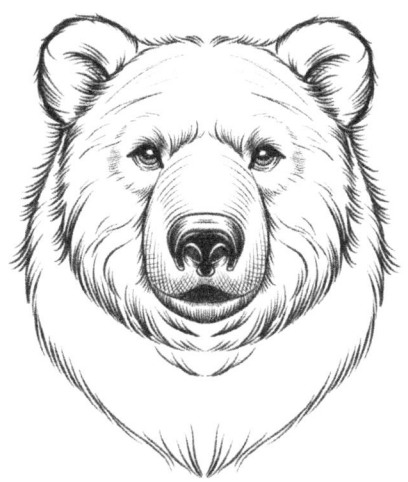

12

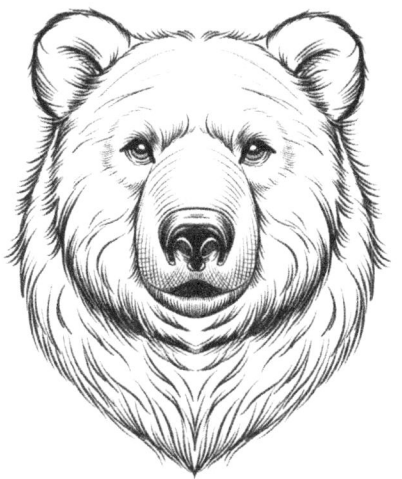

RABBIT

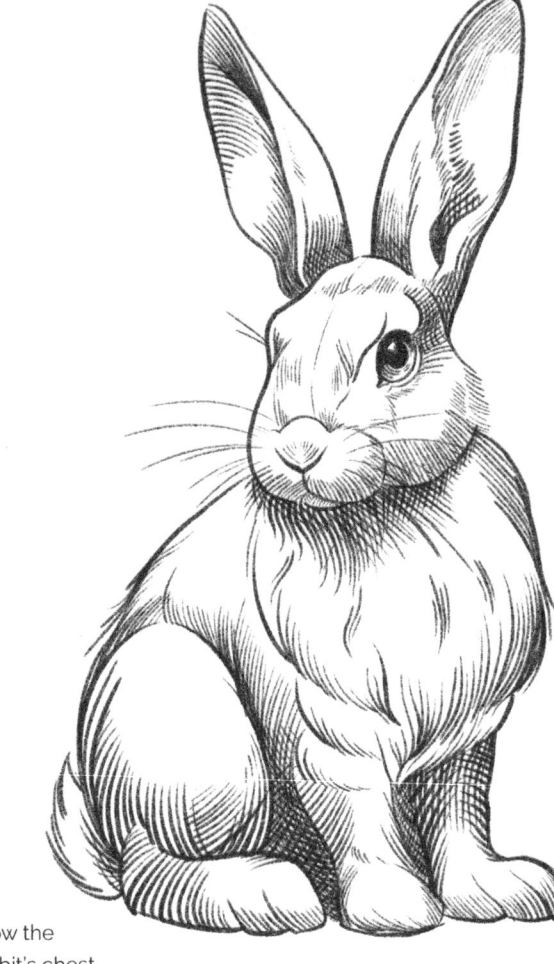

Pro Tip:
In step 04, the oval drawn below the head that will make up the rabbit's chest should approximately align to the left of the muzzle or snout.

01

02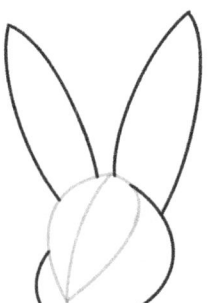

03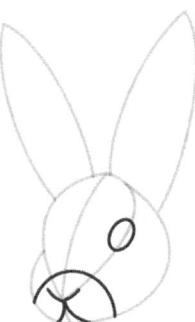

VOLUME.1 A STEP-BY-STEP GUIDE 10

04
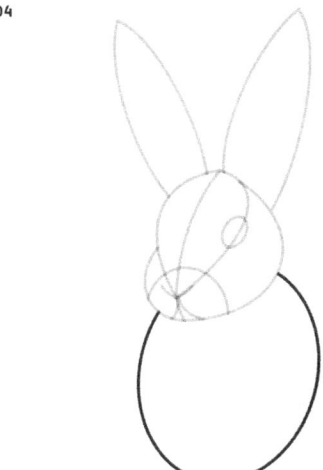

05
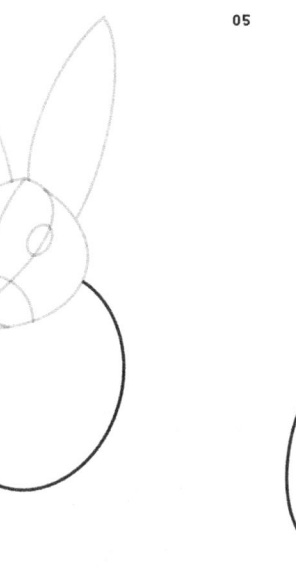

06
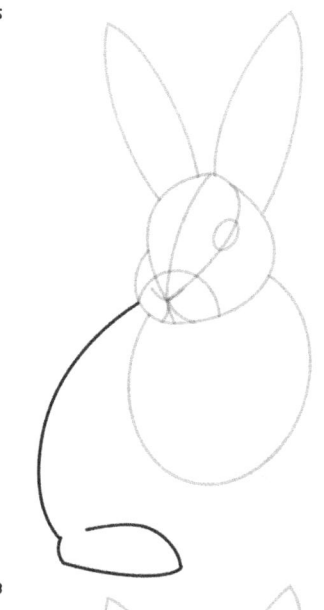

07
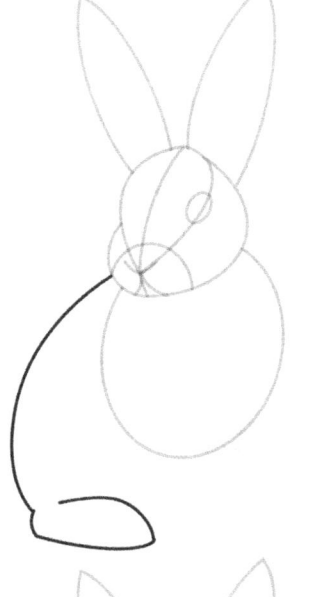

08
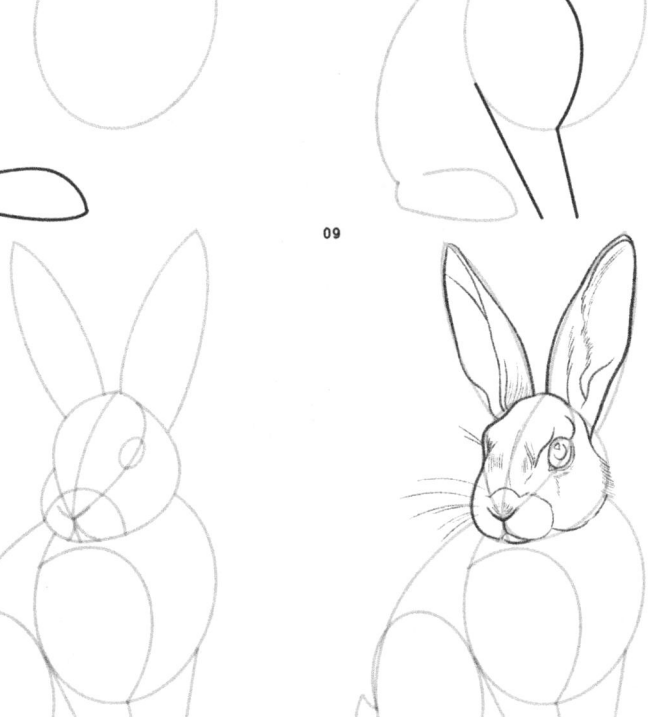

09

10
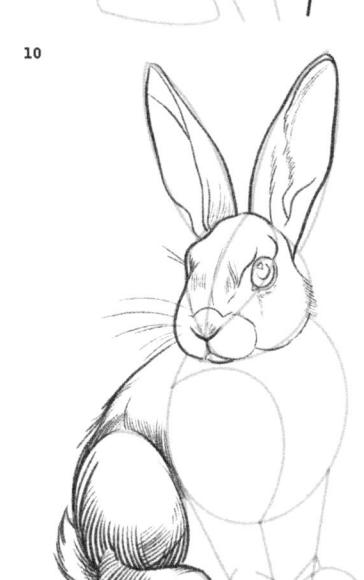

11
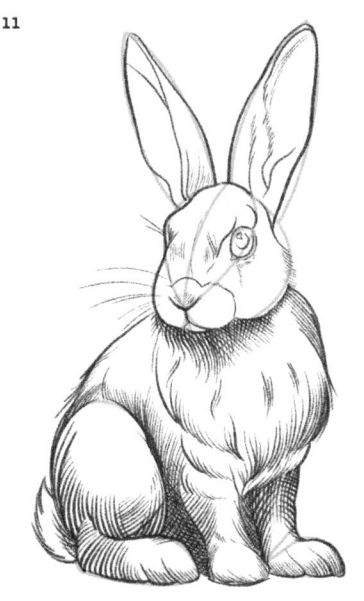

12
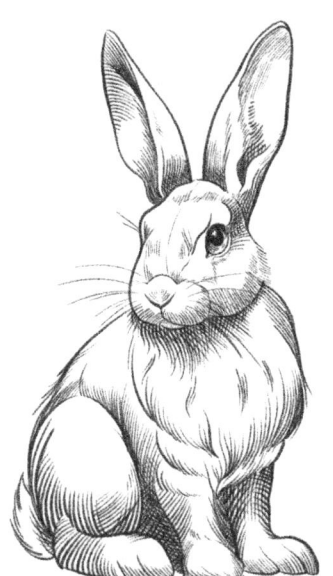

HOW TO DRAW ANIMALS

LION

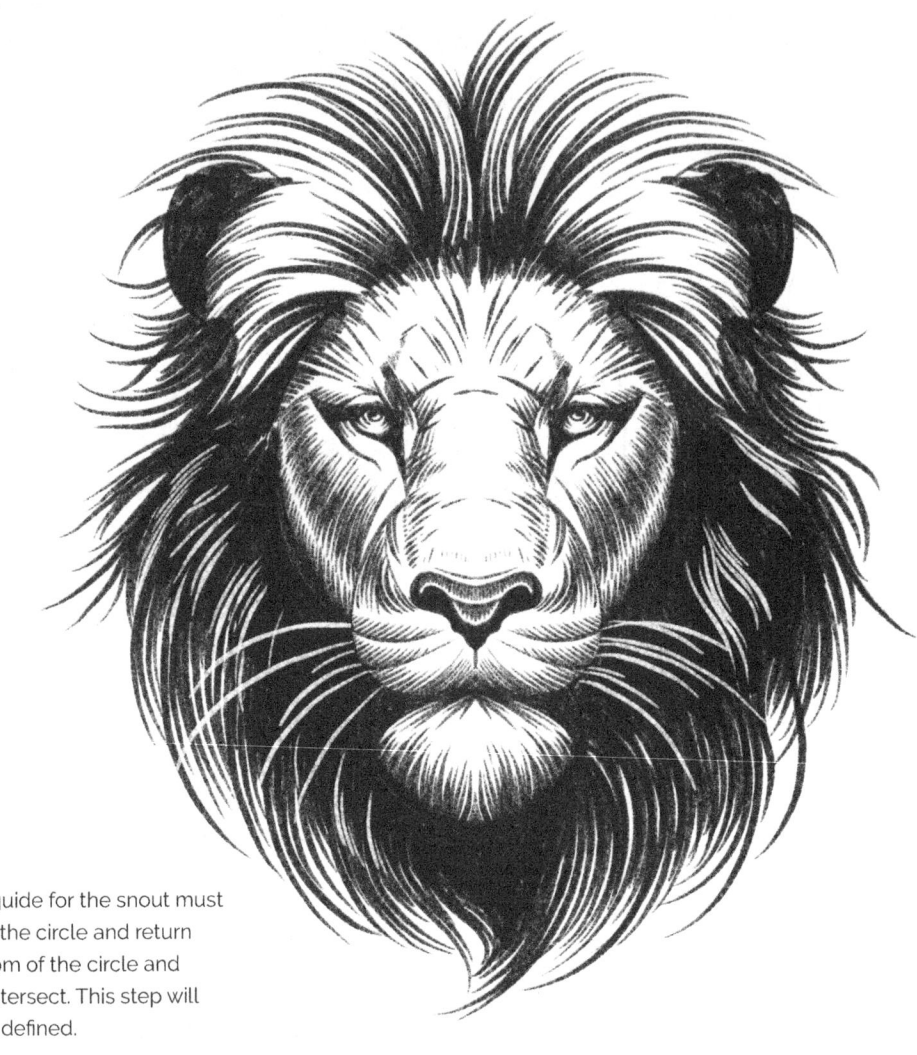

Pro Tip:
In step 03, the guide for the snout must slightly overlap the circle and return where the bottom of the circle and vertical guide intersect. This step will ensure it is well defined.

01 02 03

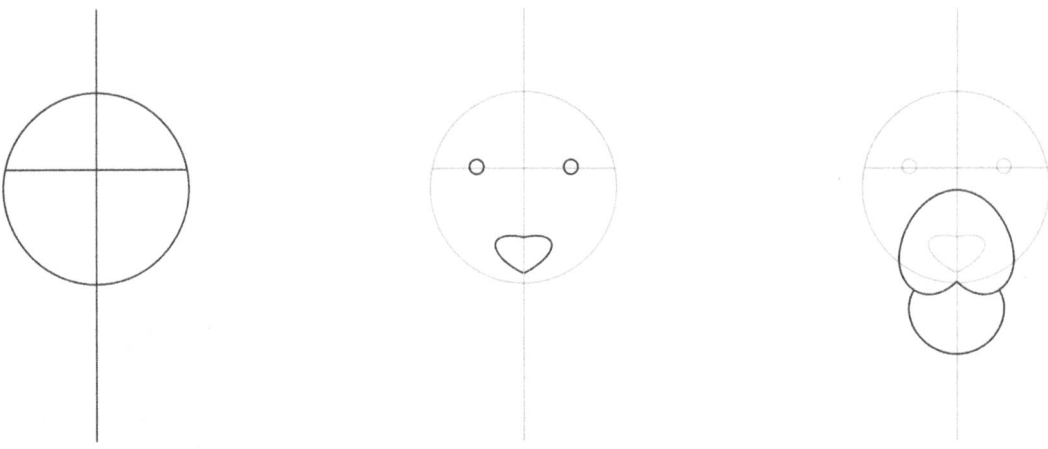

VOLUME.1　　　　　　　　　　　　　　　　　　　　　　　　　A STEP-BY-STEP GUIDE　　12

04

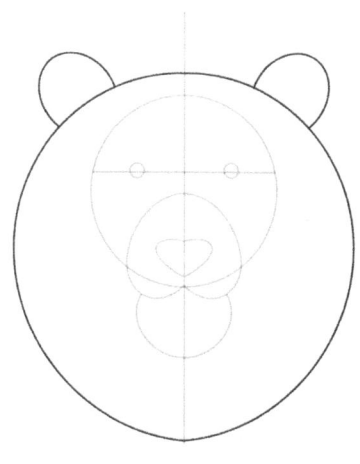

05

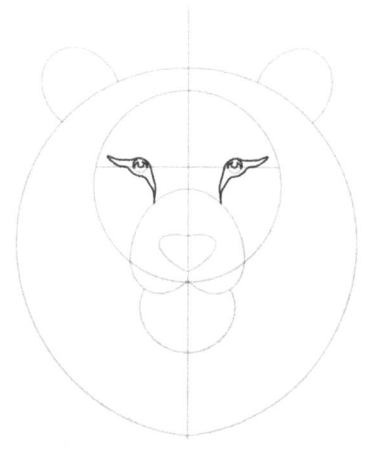

06

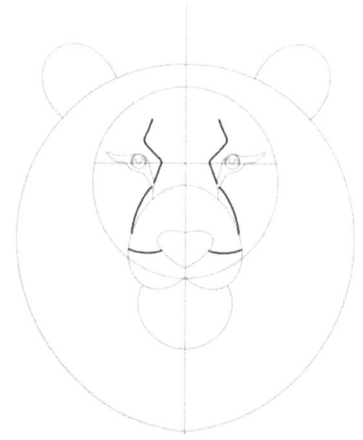

07

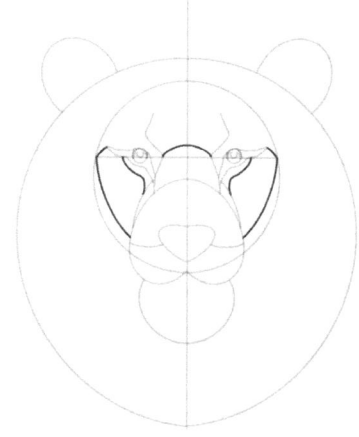

08

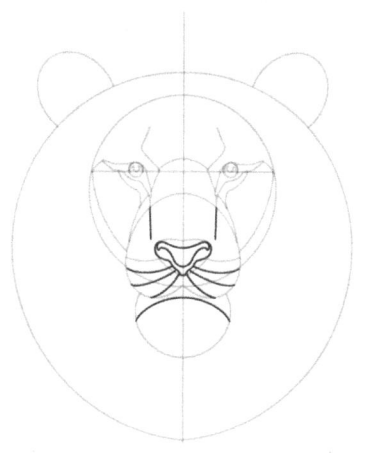

09

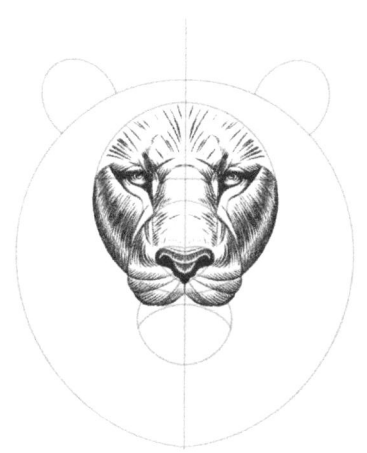

10

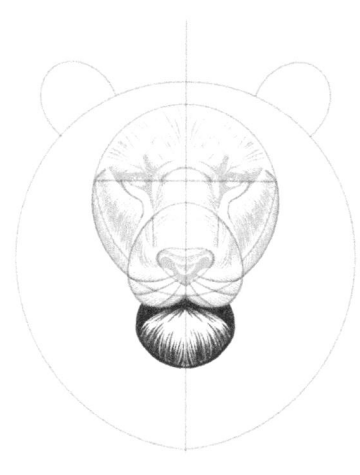

11

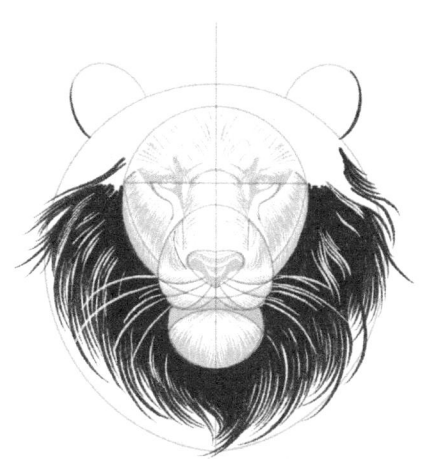

12

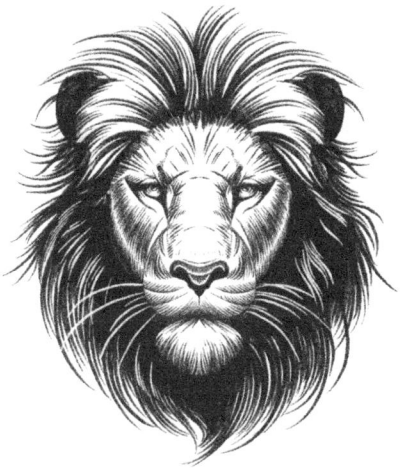

HOW TO DRAW ANIMALS

VAULTEDITIONS.COM

BAT

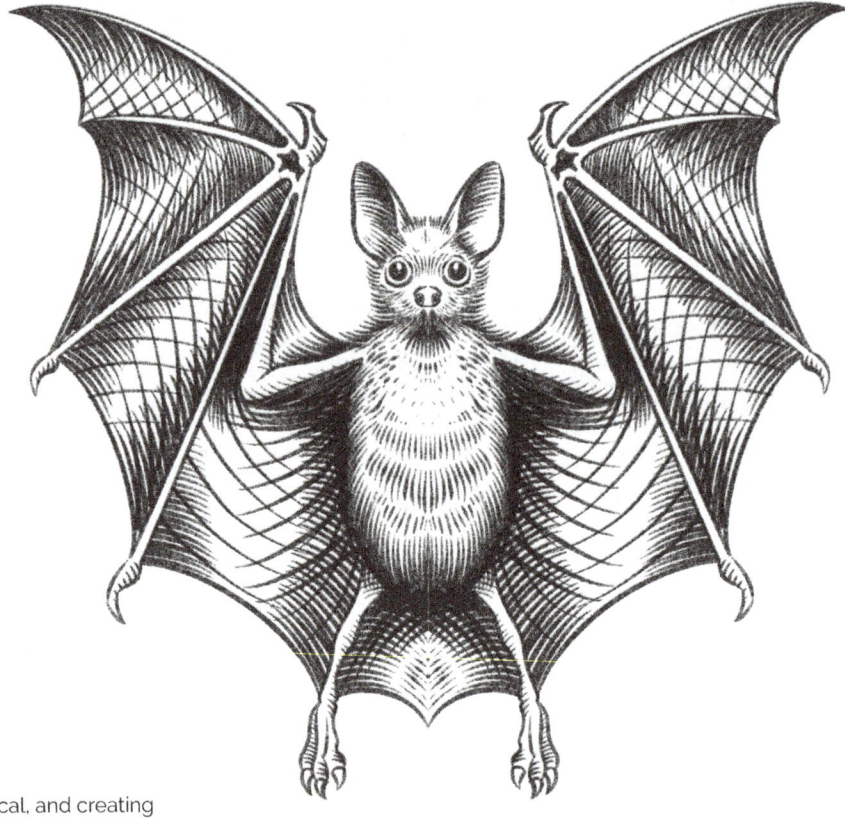

Pro Tip:
The bat is symmetrical, and creating slight variations in the line work and rendering between the left and right sides of the face provides a more natural appearance. Apply this to the body also.

01

02

03

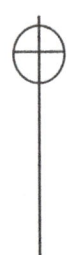
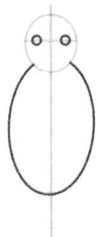
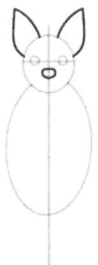

VOLUME.1　　　　　　　　　　　　　　　　　　　　A STEP-BY-STEP GUIDE

04

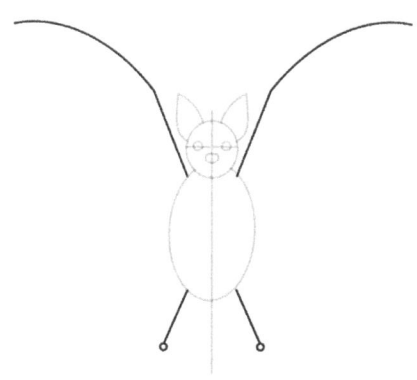

05

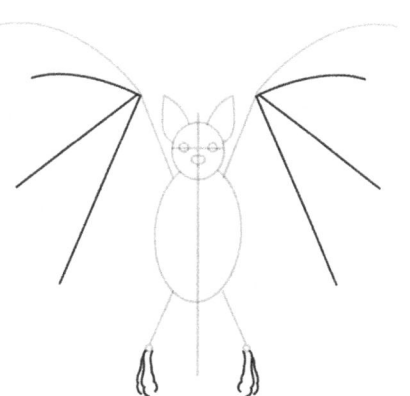

06

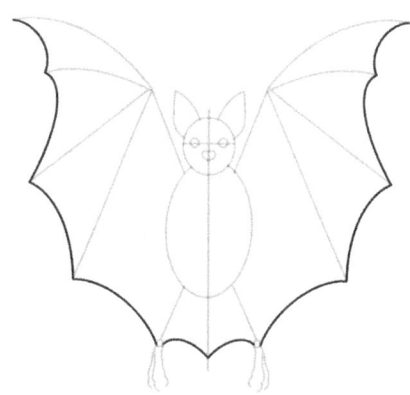

07

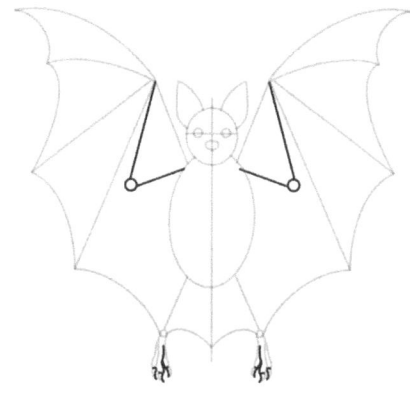

08

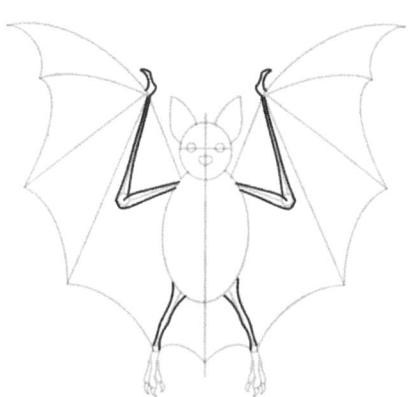

09

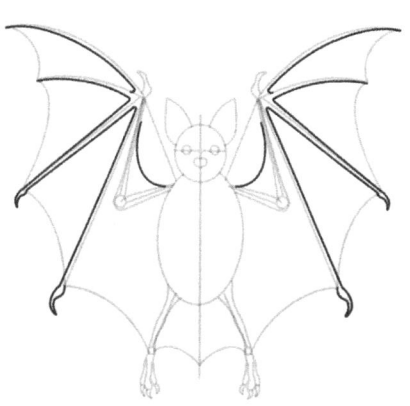

10

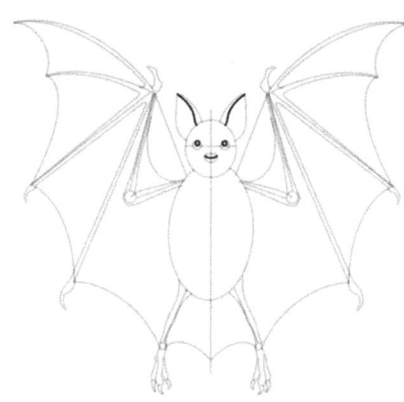

11

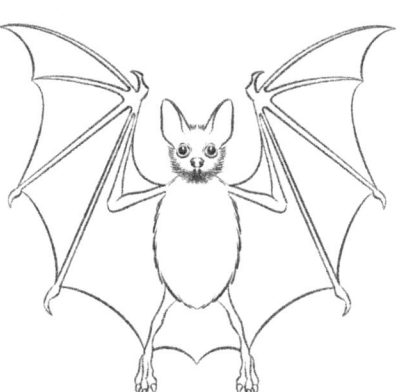

12

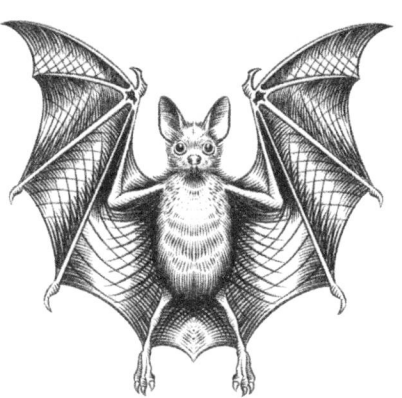

VAULTEDITIONS.COM

BISON

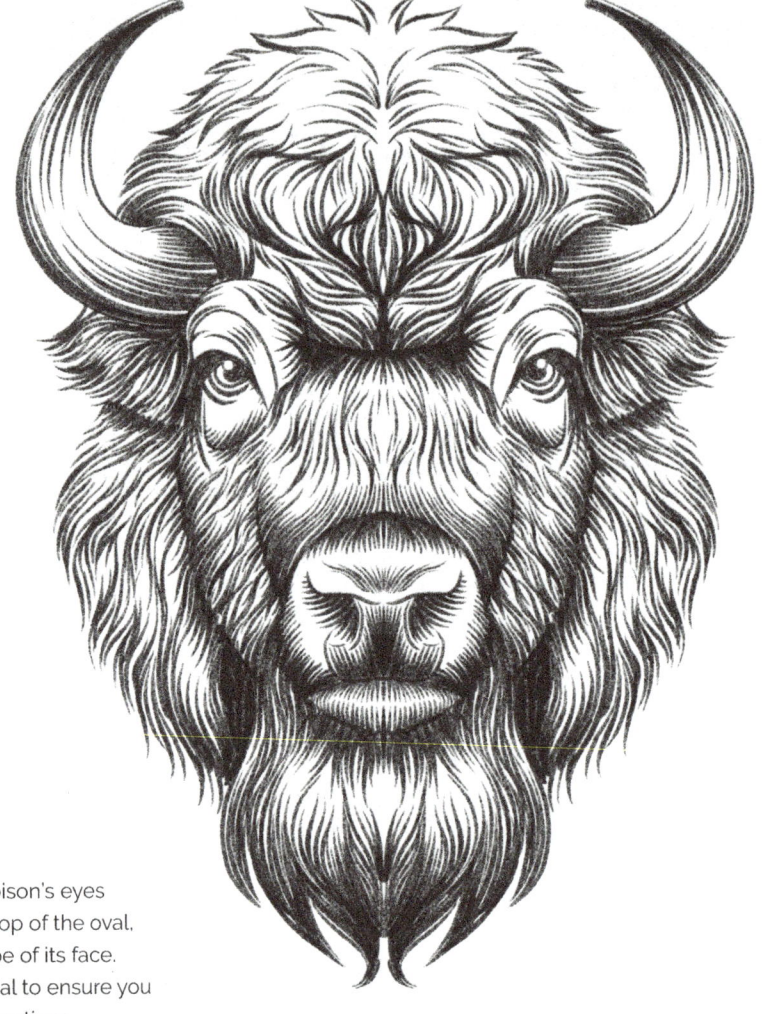

Pro Tip:
In step 01, note that the bison's eyes are located towards the top of the oval, which will guide the shape of its face. Replicating this is essential to ensure you will have the correct proportions.

01

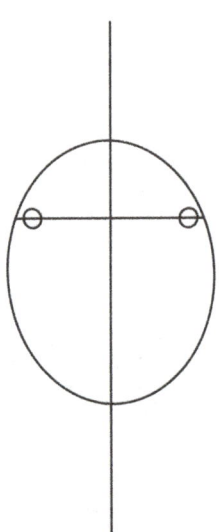

02

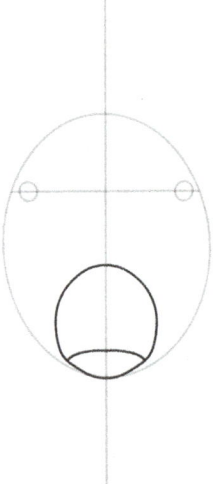

03

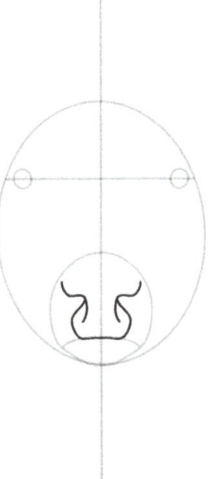

04

05

06

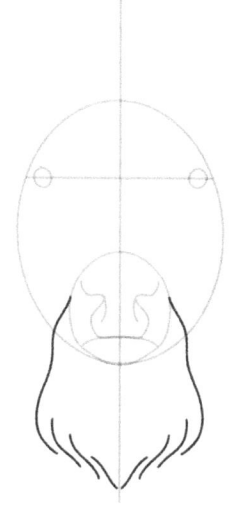
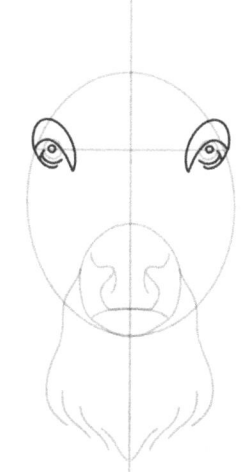
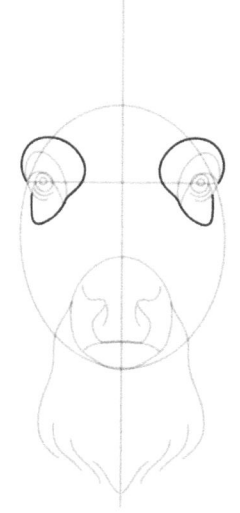

07

08

09

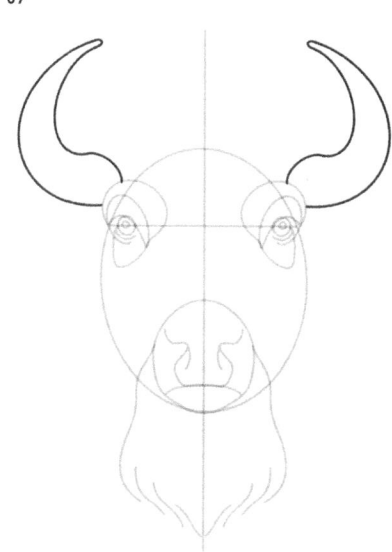
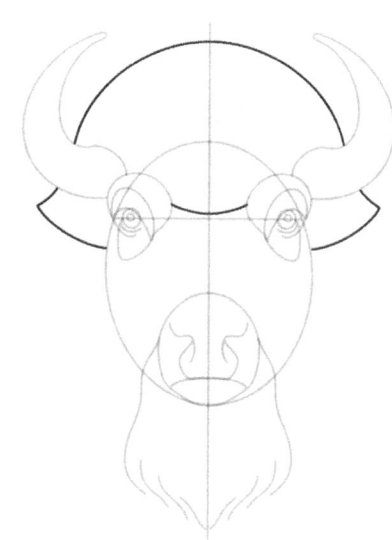
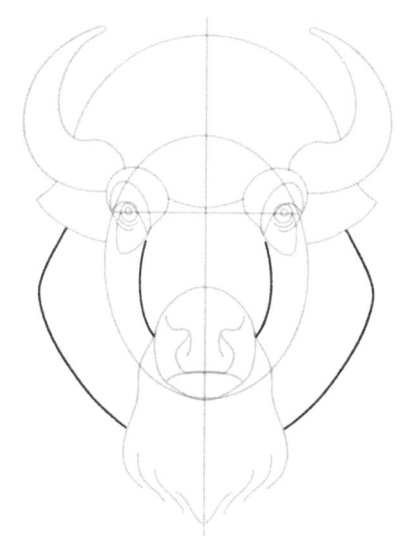

10

11

12

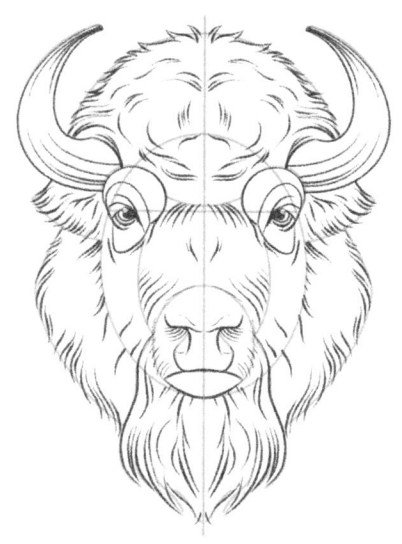
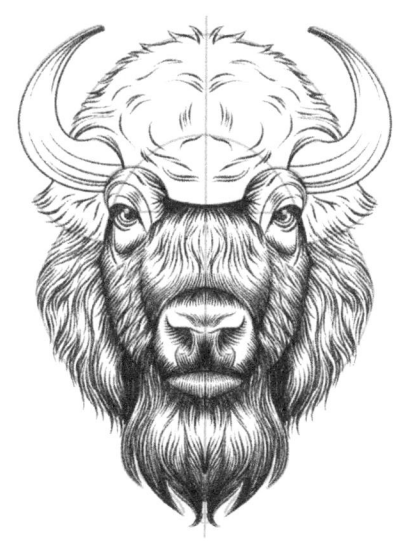
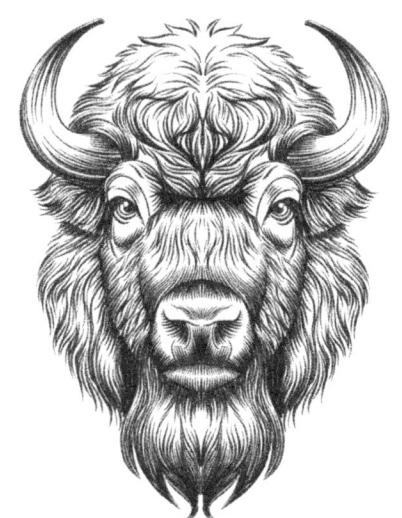

BEAR

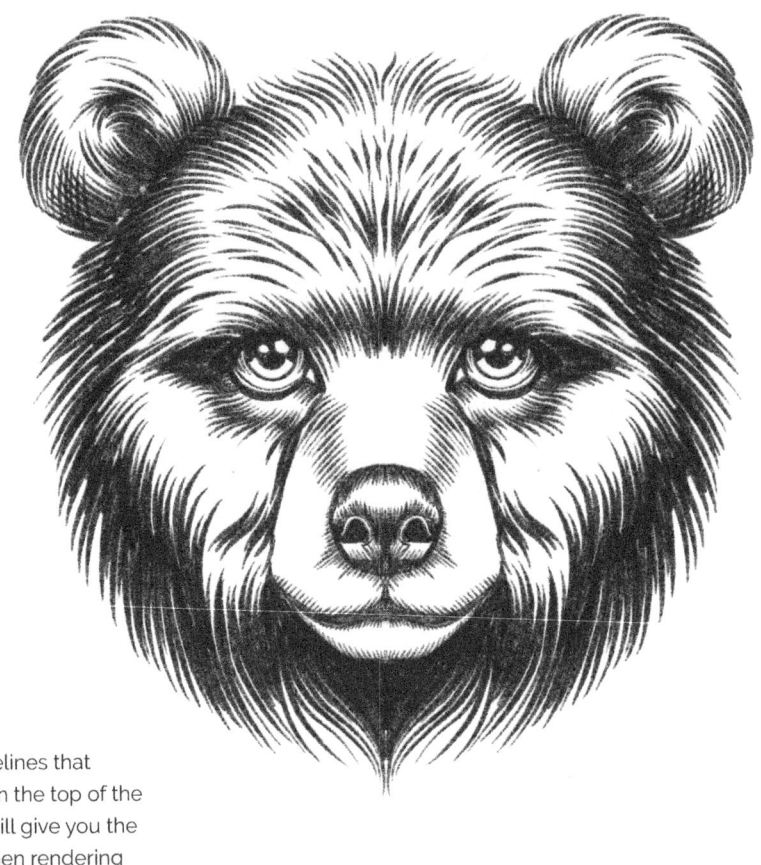

Pro Tip:
In step 06, note the guidelines that connect the eye duct with the top of the nose. Marking this area will give you the guides you need later when rendering the artwork to correctly define the shape of the snout.

01

02

03

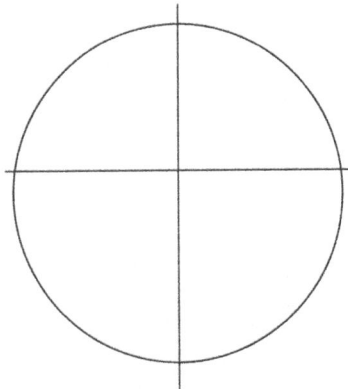

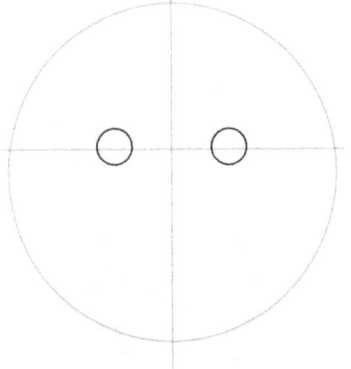

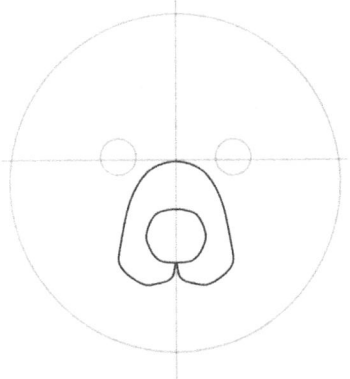

04
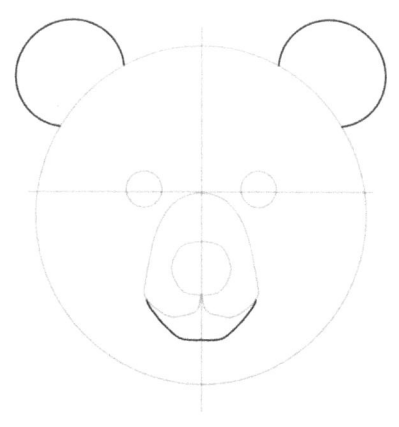

05
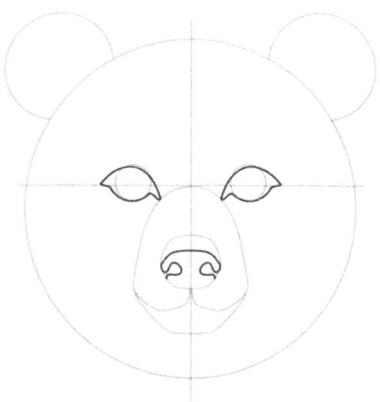

06
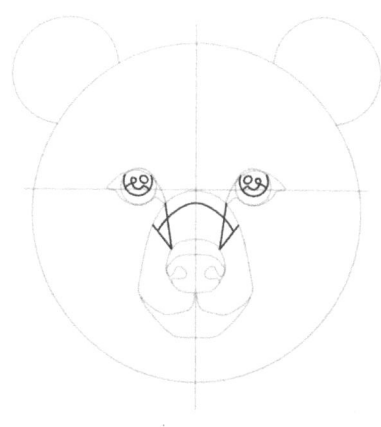

07
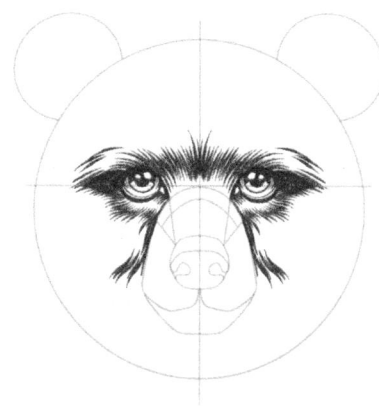

08
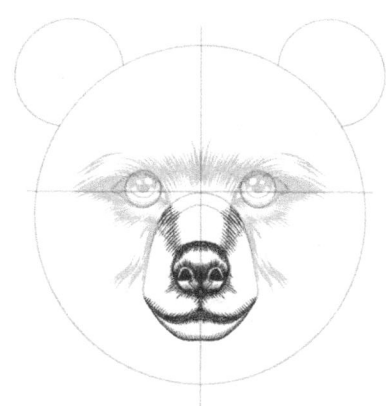

09
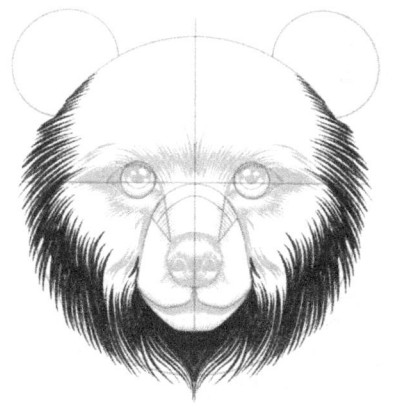

10
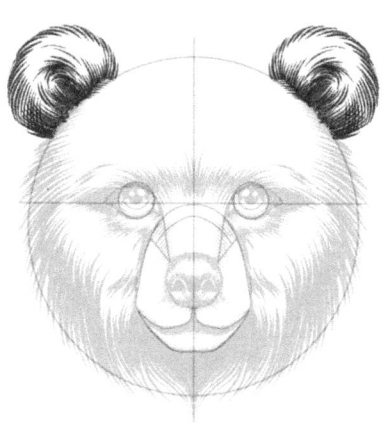

11
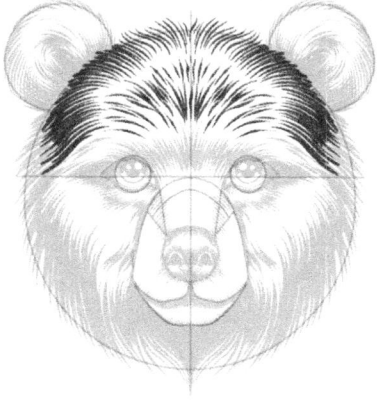

12
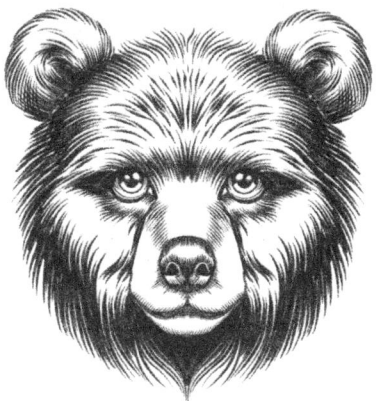

BEAVER

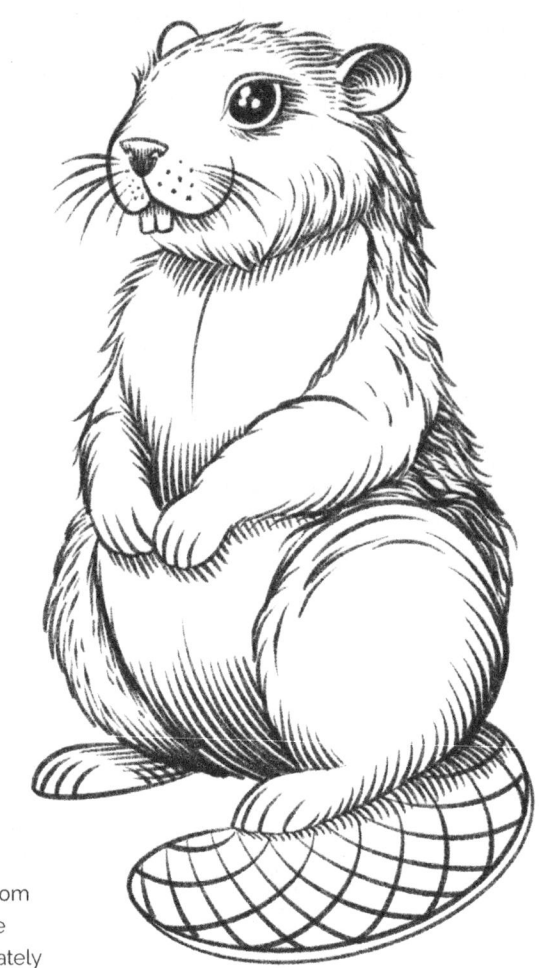

Pro Tip:
In step 01, the line that descends from the oval guide that will make up the beaver's head should be approximately 3.5 times the size of that oval.

01

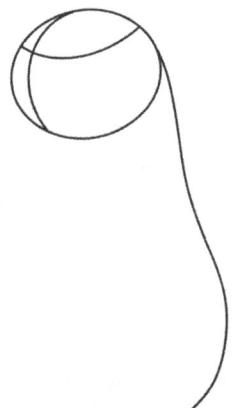

02

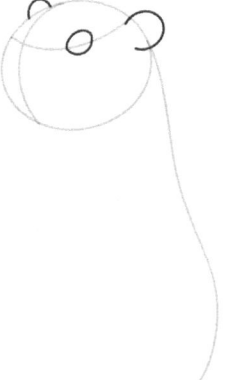

03

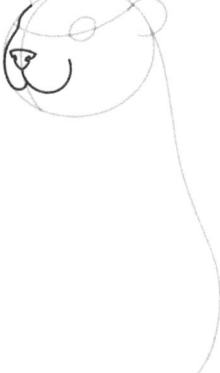

VOLUME.1　　　　　　　　　　　　　　　　　　　　　　A STEP-BY-STEP GUIDE　　20

04
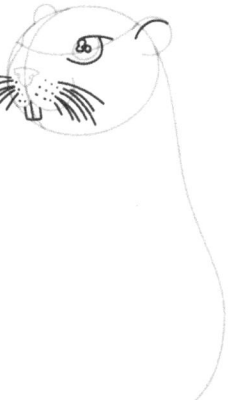

05
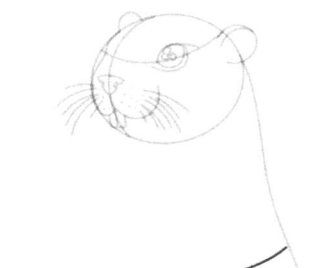

06
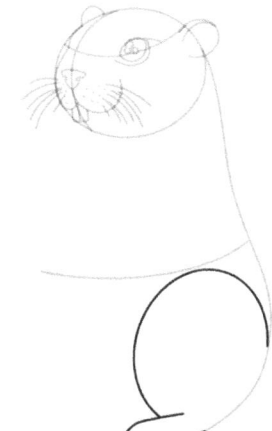

07
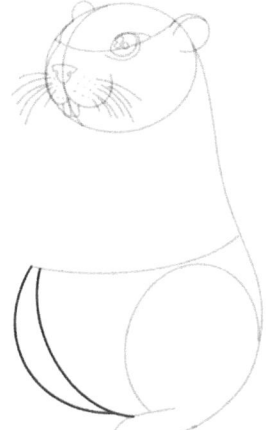

08
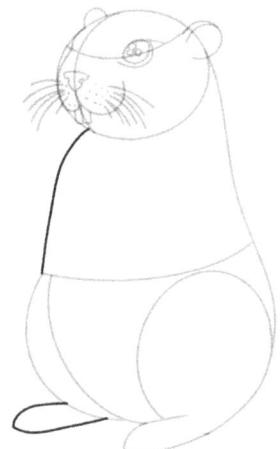

09
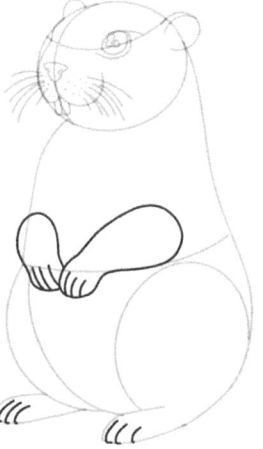

10
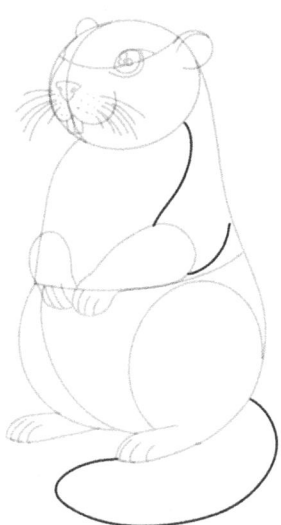

11
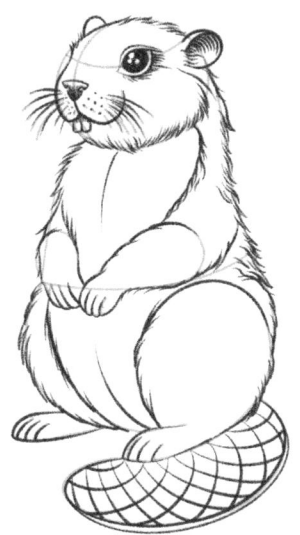

12
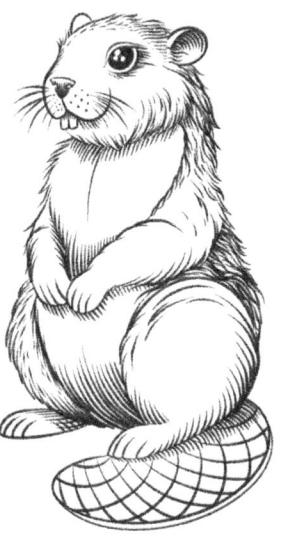

HOW TO DRAW ANIMALS

VAULTEDITIONS.COM

BUTTERFLY

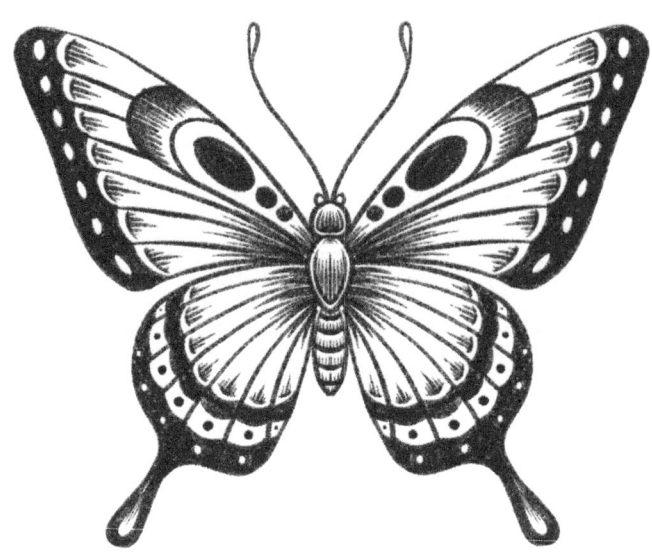

Pro Tip:
Shading the wings on either side of the butterfly's body helps to define its form and differentiate the various parts of the insect's body.

01

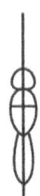

02

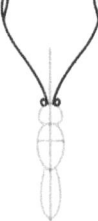

03

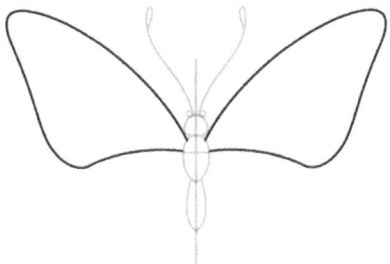

04

05

06

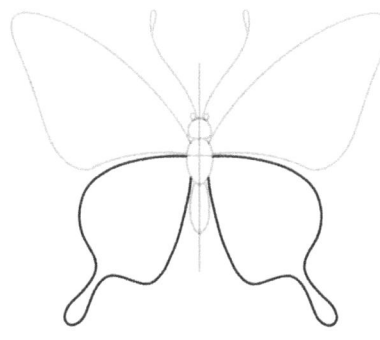
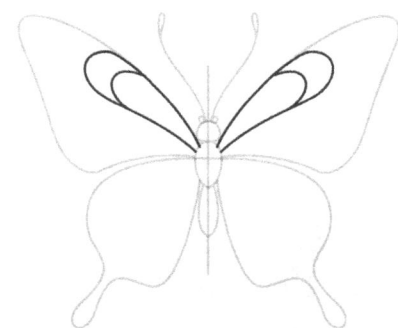
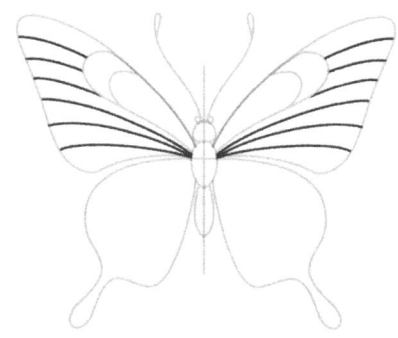

07

08

09

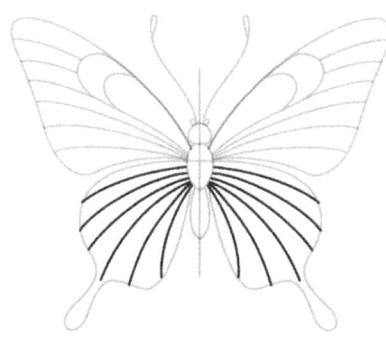
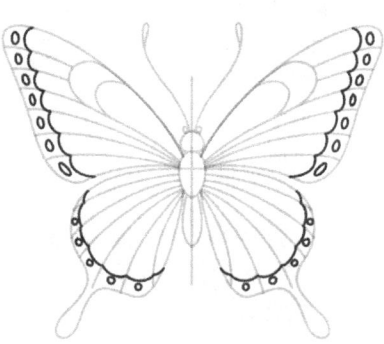
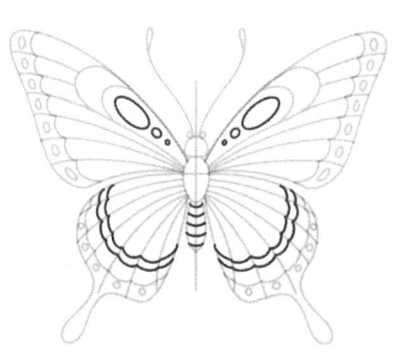

10

11

12

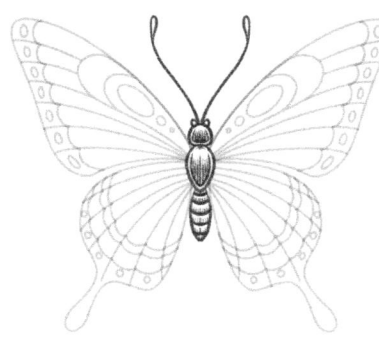
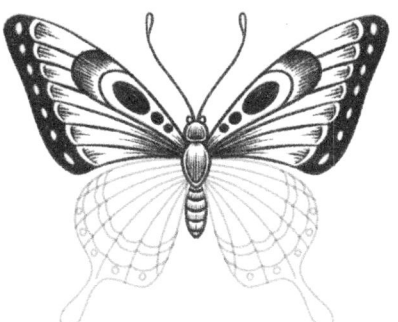
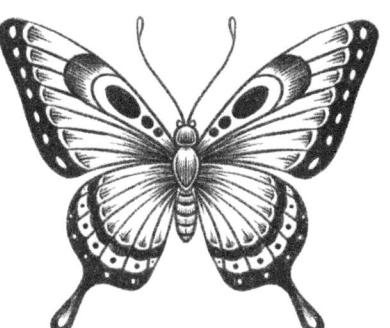

CAT

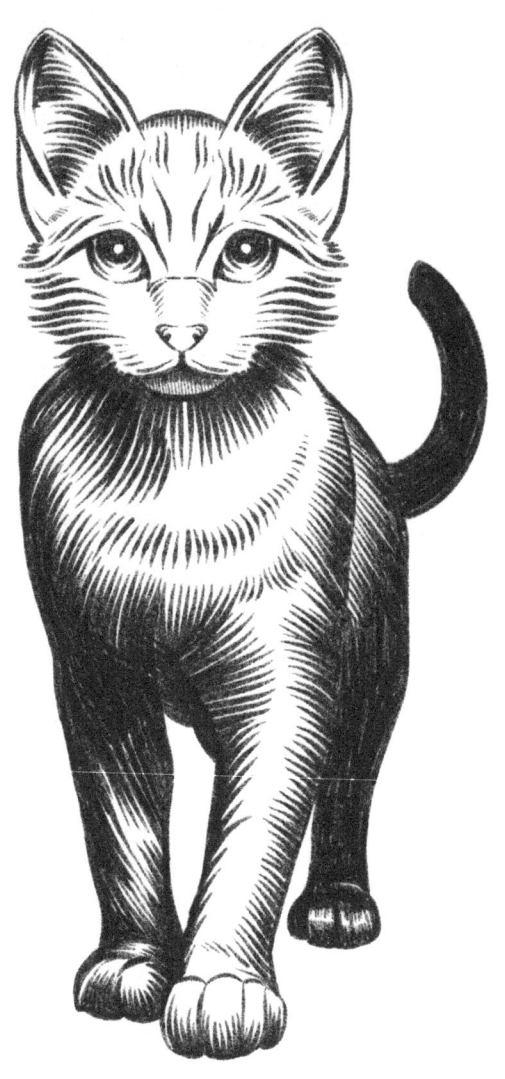

Pro Tip:
When determining the height of the leg in step 07, note that it is approximately the exact height of the torso and head combined, excluding the ears.

01

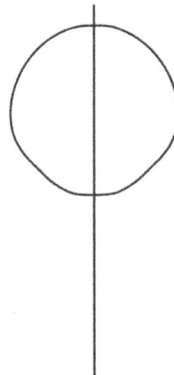

02

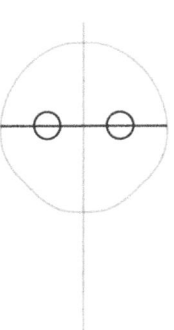

03

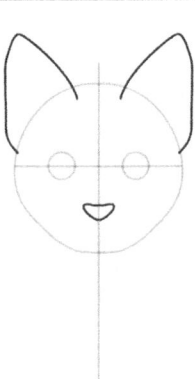

04

05

06

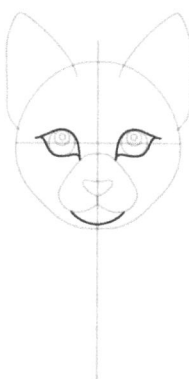
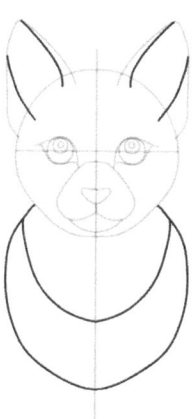

07

08

09

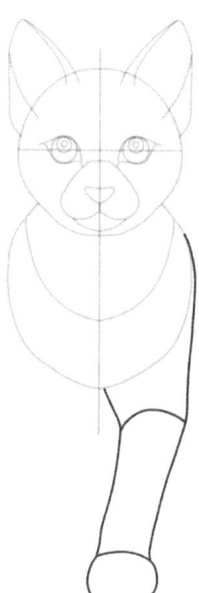
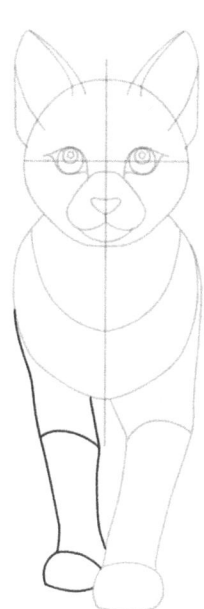
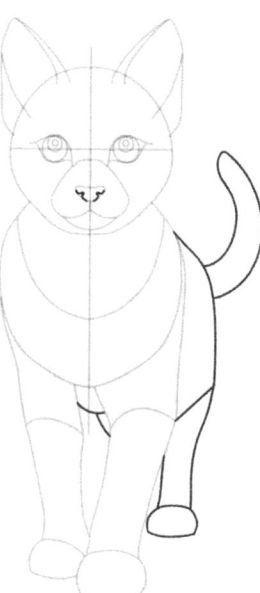

10

11

12

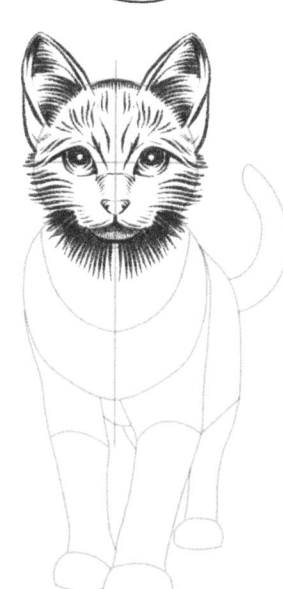
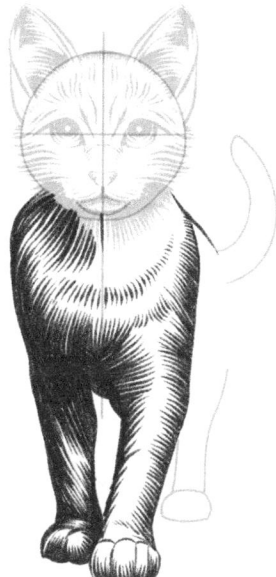
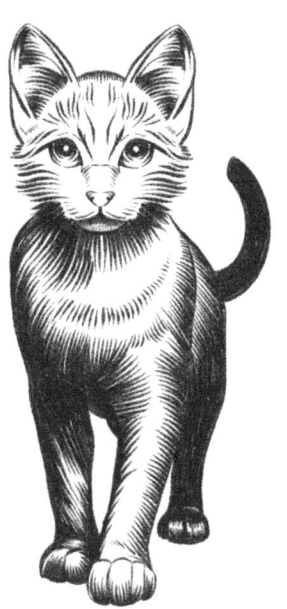

DOG'S HEAD

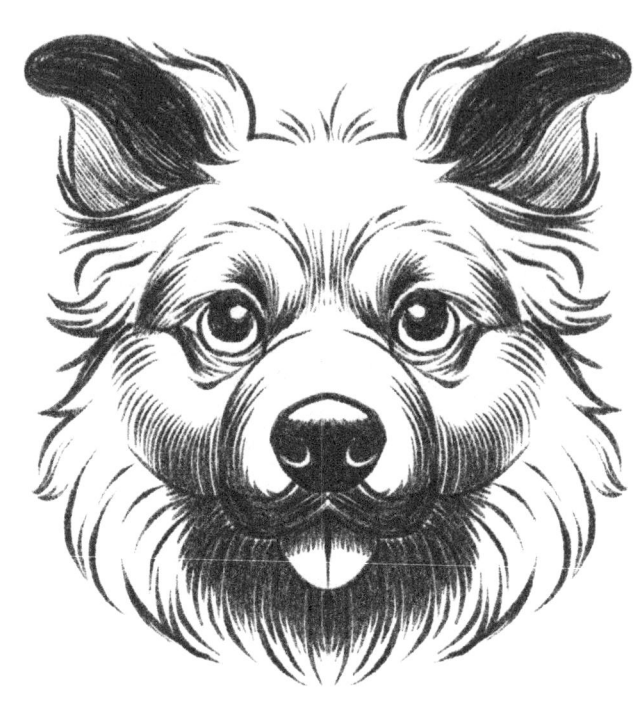

Pro Tip:
In step 09, note the heavy shading under the tongue and muzzle. This helps define the shape of the dog's face and prevents it from blending with the hair on the upper torso.

01

02

03

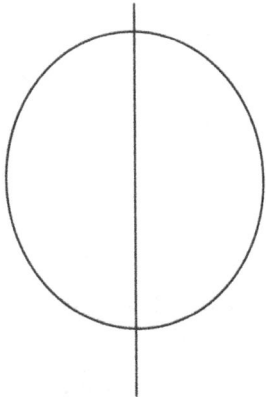
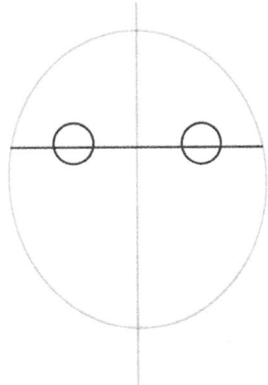
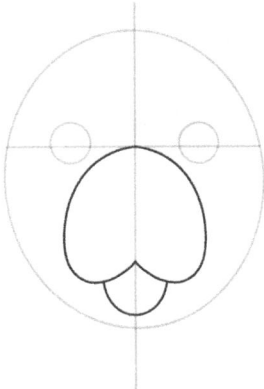

VOLUME.1
A STEP-BY-STEP GUIDE

04
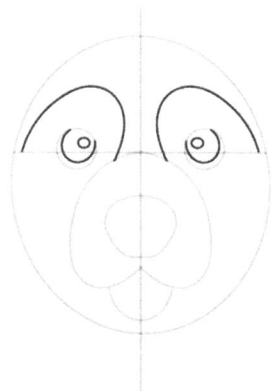

05
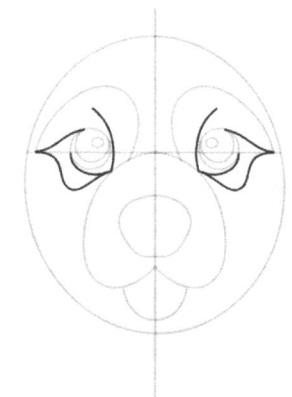

06
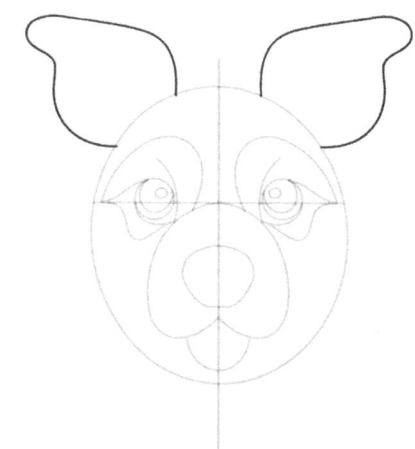

07
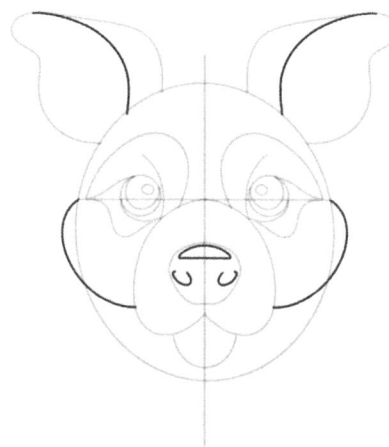

08
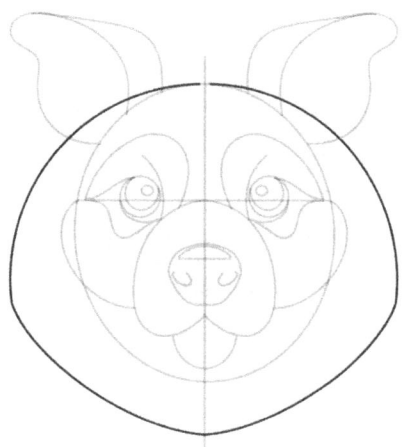

09
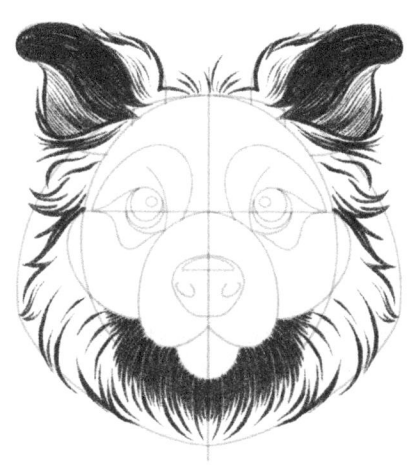

10
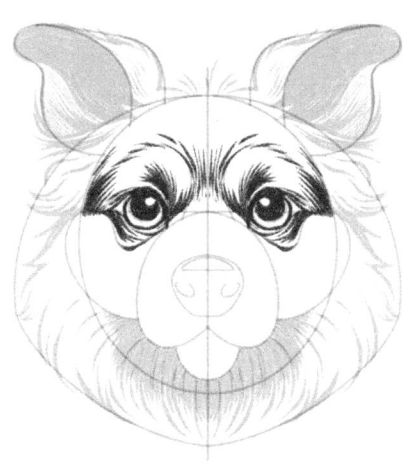

11
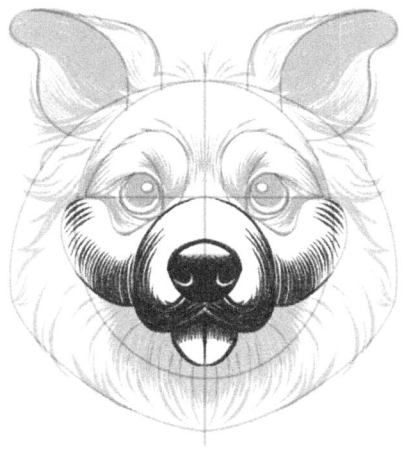

12
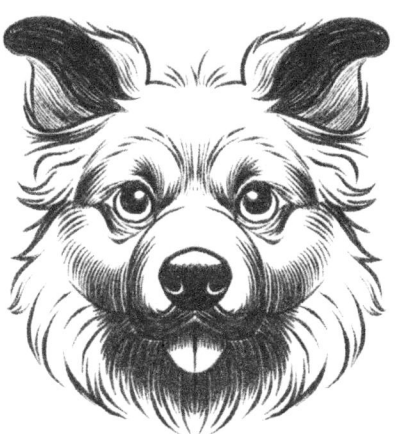

HOW TO DRAW ANIMALS

VAULTEDITIONS.COM

DOBERMAN

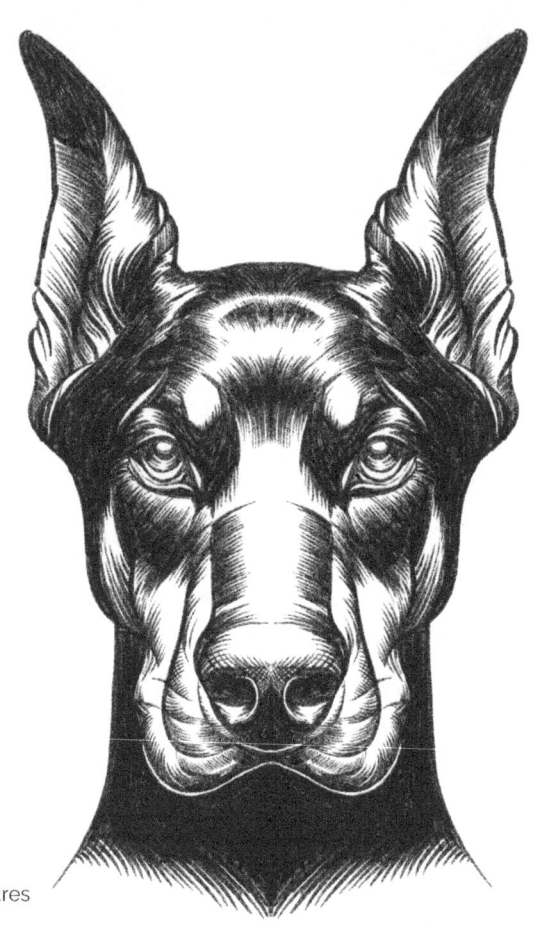

Pro Tip:
One of the Doberman's defining features is its striking, pointed ears. Note that they are approximately the height of the circular guide and begin just before the horizontal axis.

01

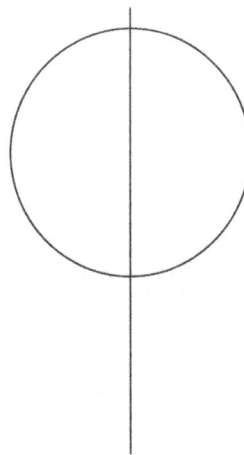

02

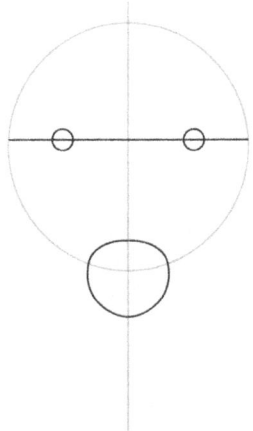

03

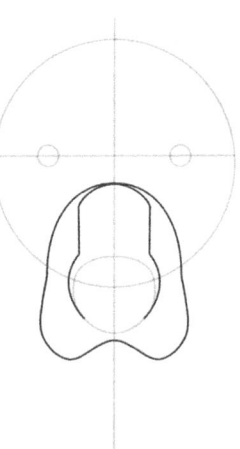

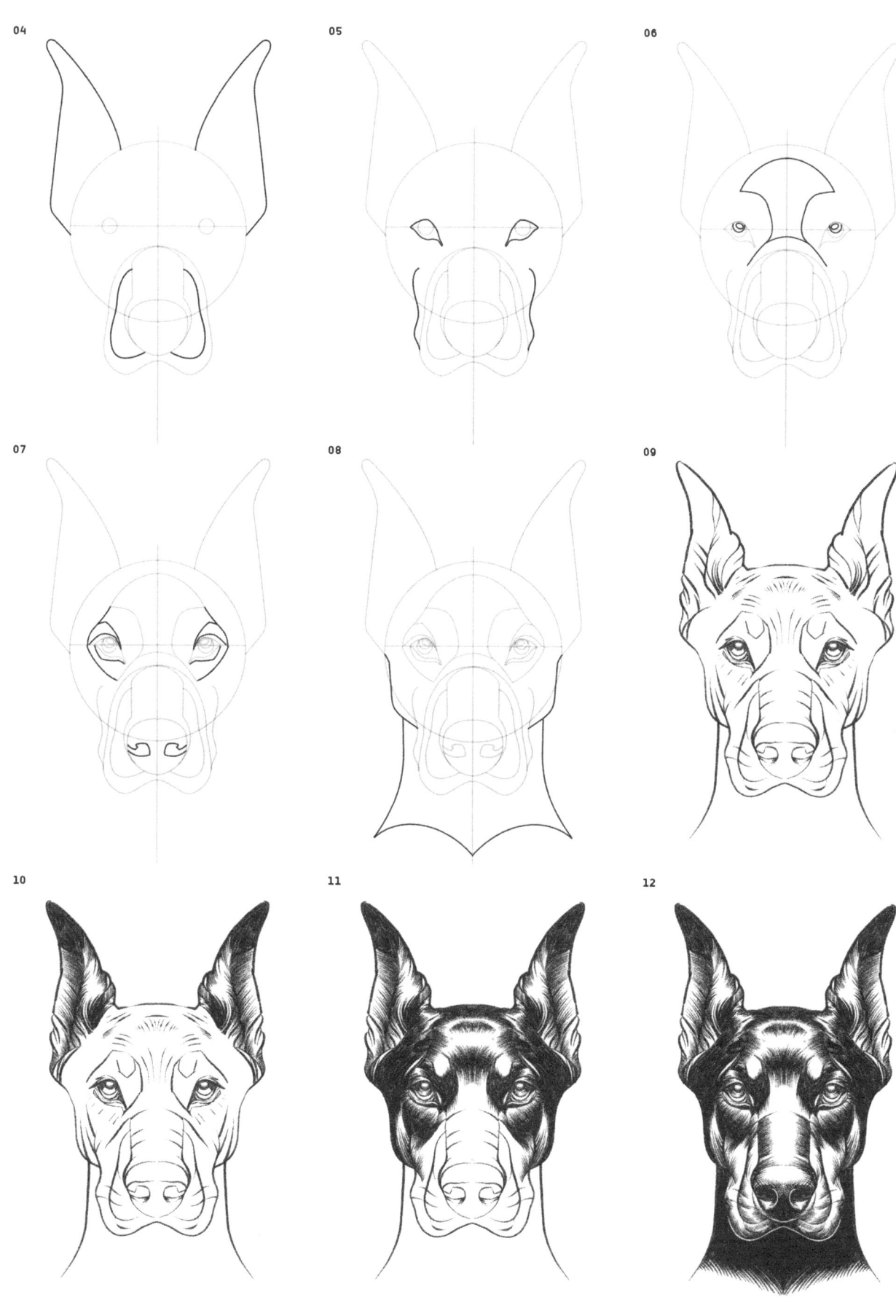

SHARK

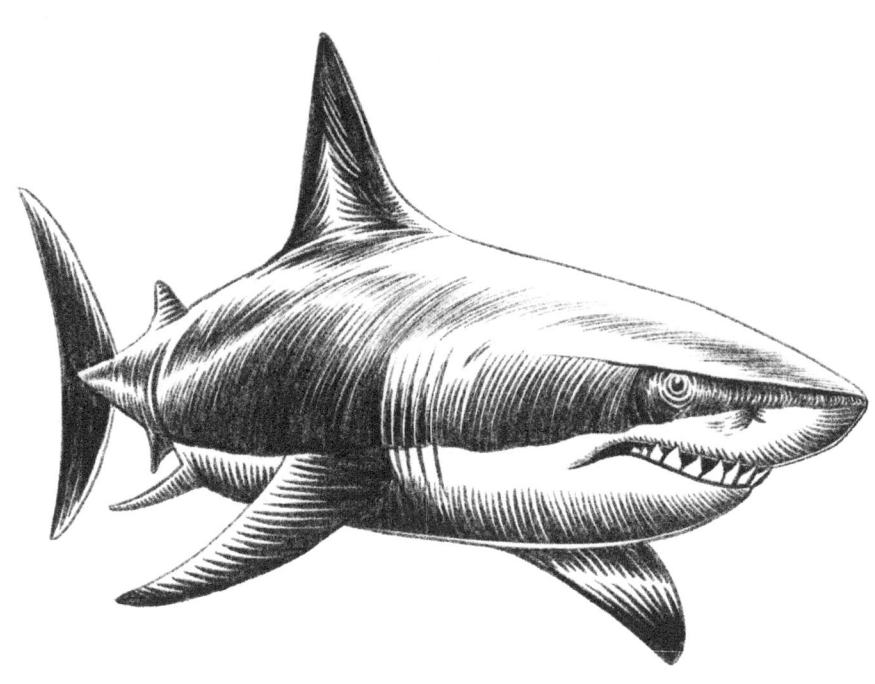

Pro Tip:
In step 01, notice that the intersection of the two lines on the left-hand side is slightly higher than on the right. Replicating this detail is key to achieving the correct perspective in this tutorial.

01

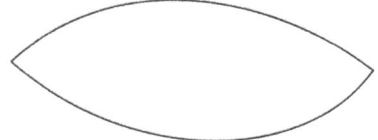

02

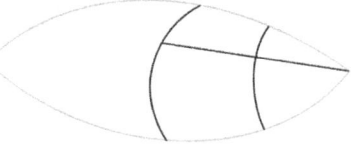

03

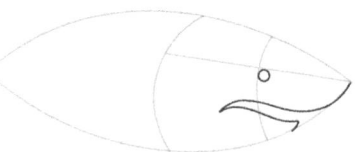

VOLUME.1　　　　　　　　　　　　　　　　　　　　　　　　A STEP-BY-STEP GUIDE

04　　　　　　　　　　　05　　　　　　　　　　　06

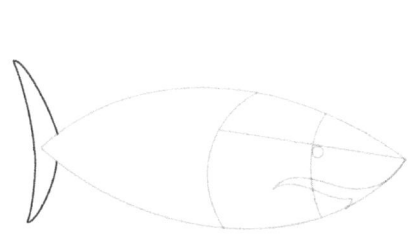 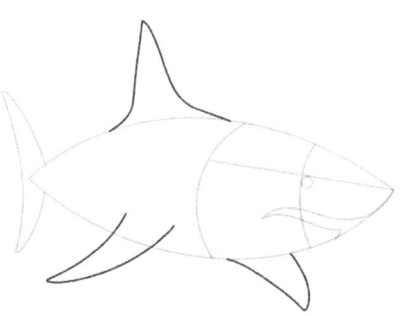 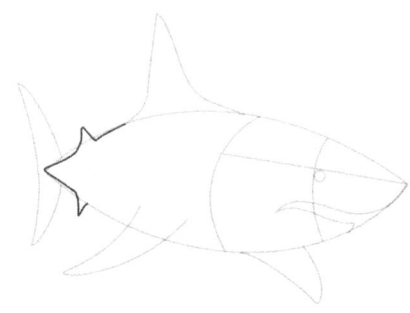

07　　　　　　　　　　　08　　　　　　　　　　　09

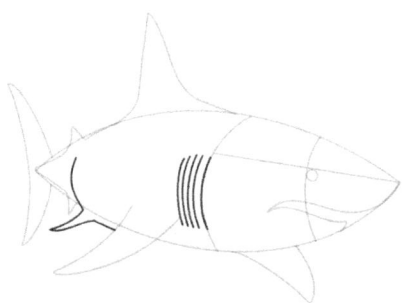 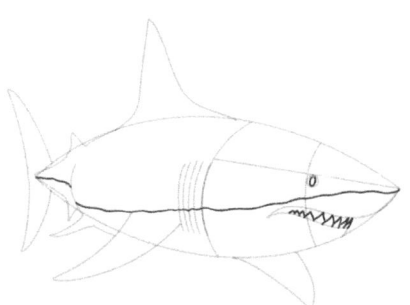 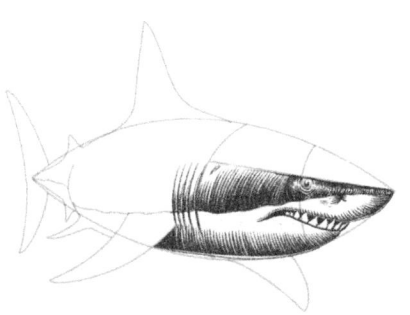

10　　　　　　　　　　　11　　　　　　　　　　　12

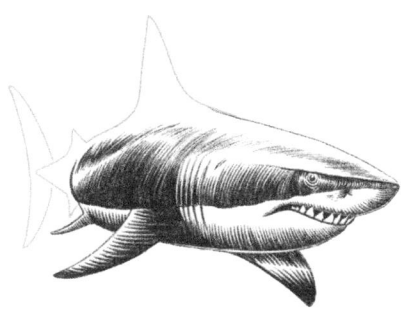 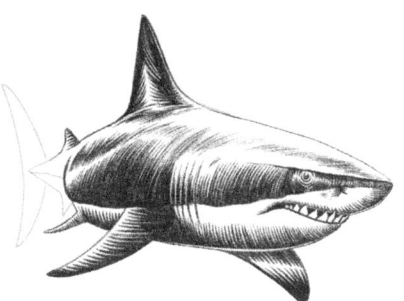 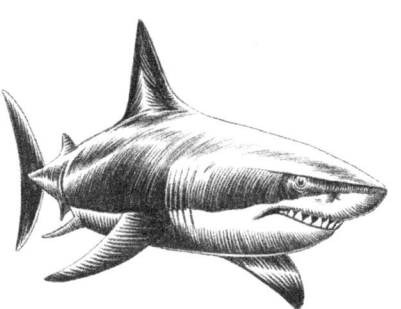

HOW TO DRAW ANIMALS

DOLPHIN

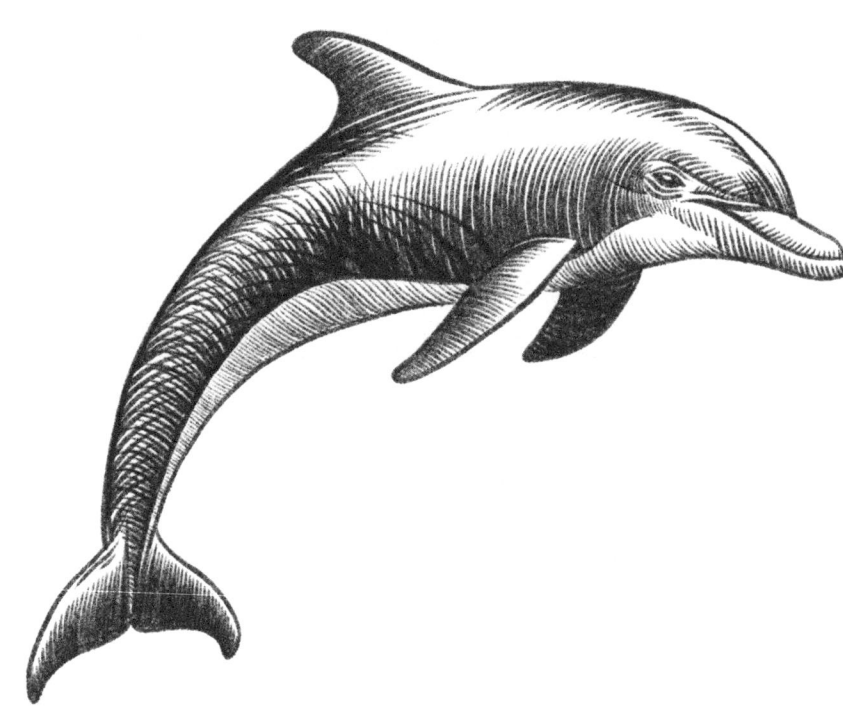

Pro Tip:
In step 02, draw the intersecting line at approximately one-third of the oval's width on the right-hand side. This detail is crucial for positioning the dolphin's eye in a natural and realistic manner.

01

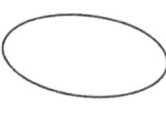

02

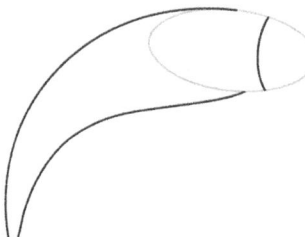

03

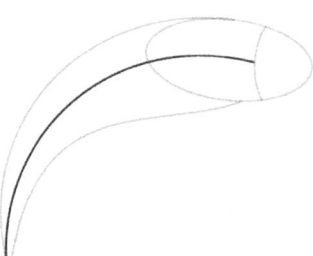

04

05

06

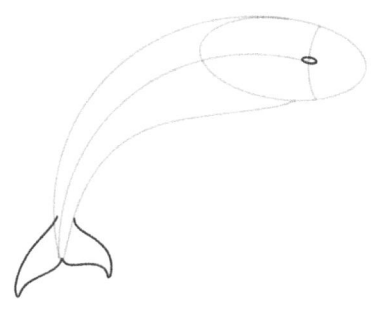
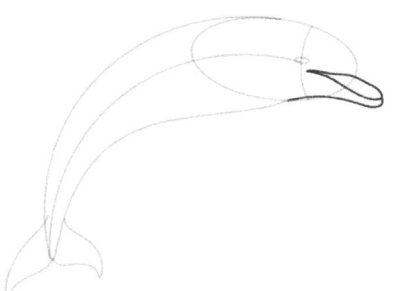
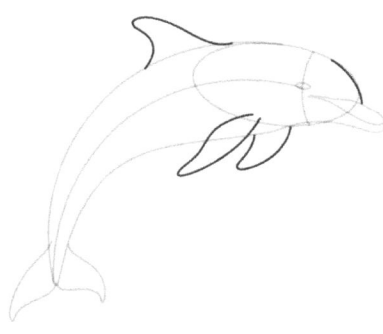

07

08

09

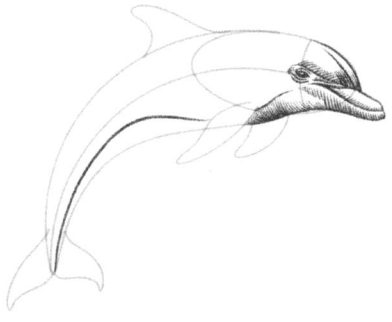
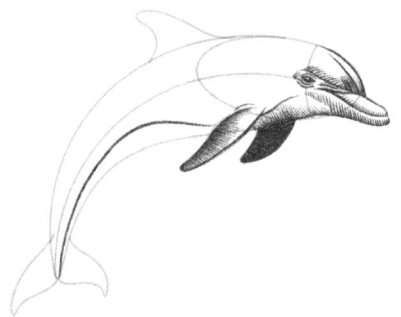
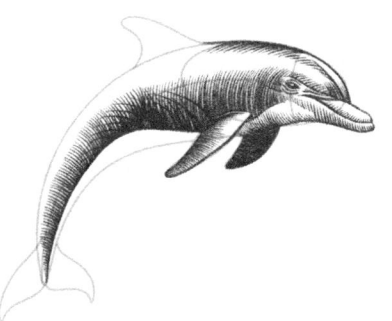

10

11

12

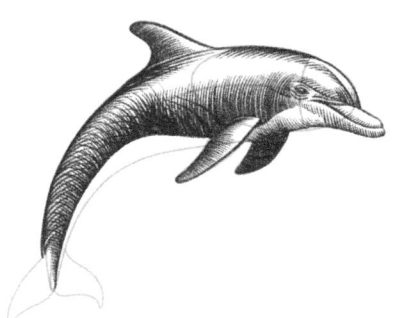
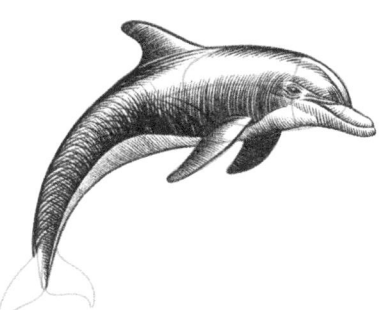
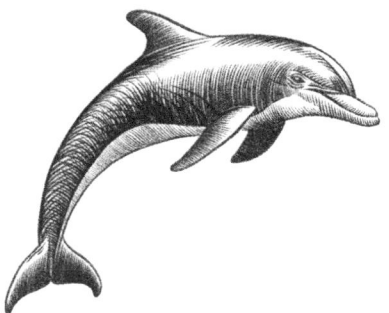

DRAGONFLY

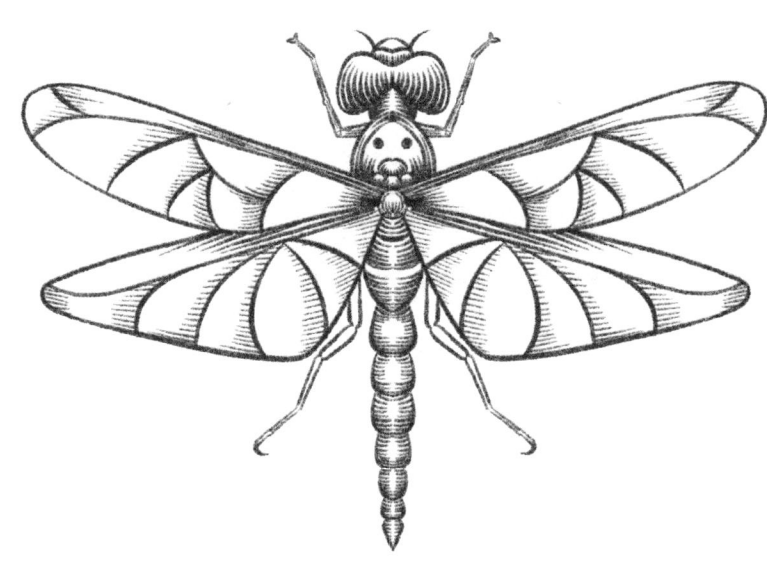

Pro Tip:
In step 11, when inking your linework and erasing the guides, pay attention to the wings closest to the head, notice they overlap the wings beneath them. Avoid inking the lower wings within the intersected area.

01

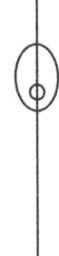

02

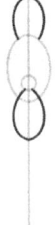

03

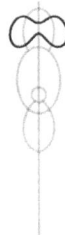

VOLUME.1   A STEP-BY-STEP GUIDE

04

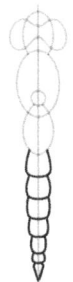

05

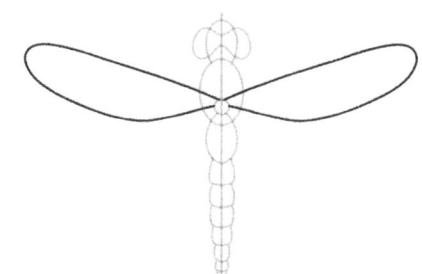

06

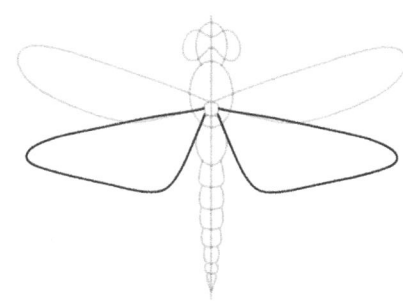

07

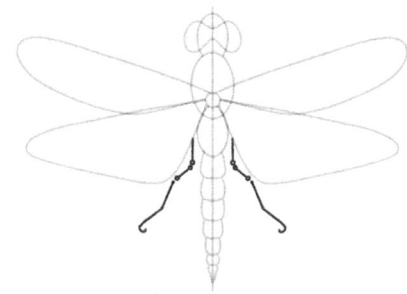

08

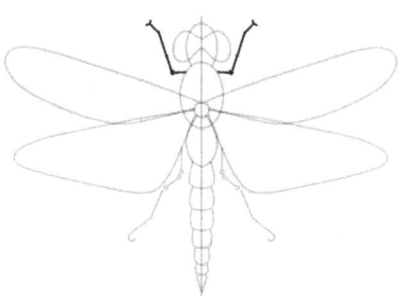

09

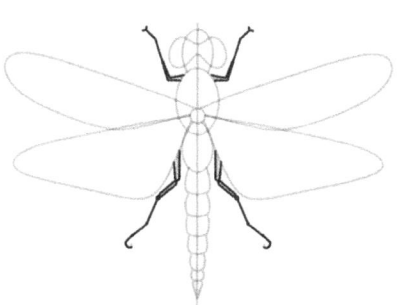

10

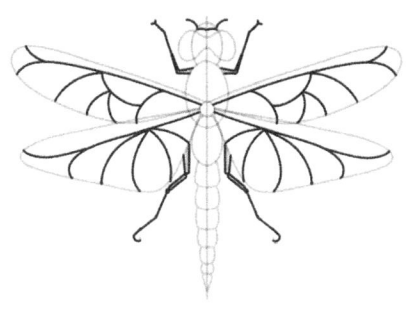

11

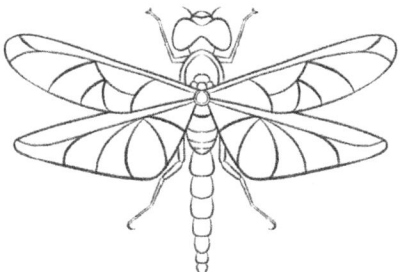

12

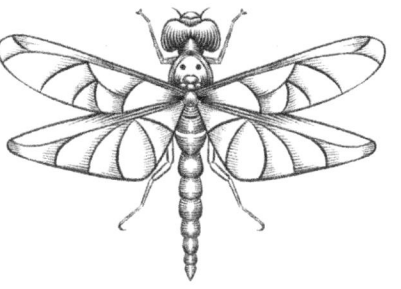

HOW TO DRAW ANIMALS

VAULTEDITIONS.COM

EAGLE

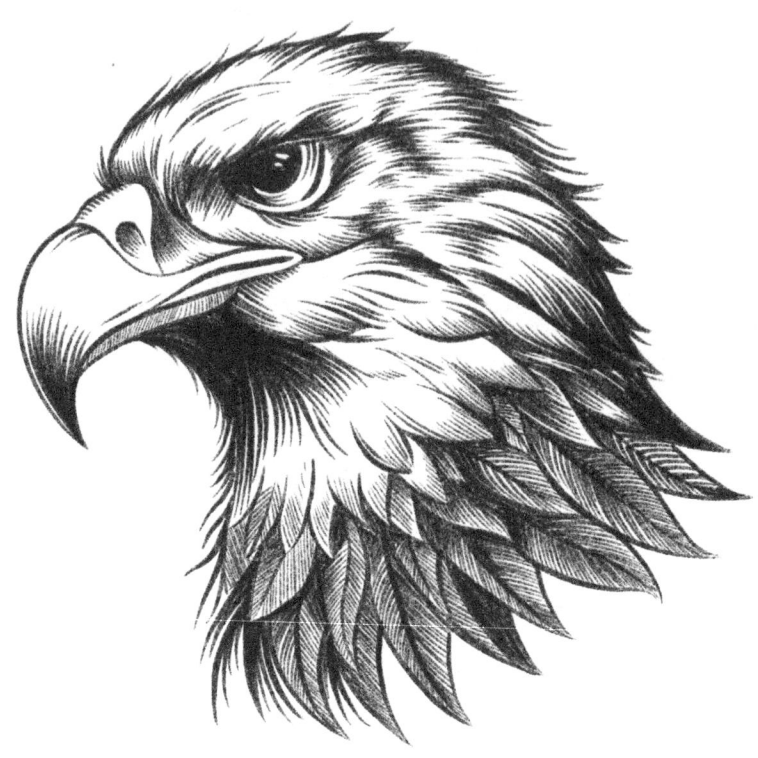

Pro Tip:
In step 03, note the eye's position and where it intersects with the cross-section of the two lines. Replicate this positioning accurately to ensure the eye's placement appears natural and proportionate.

01

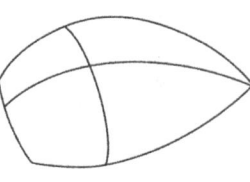

02

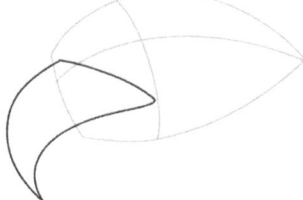

03

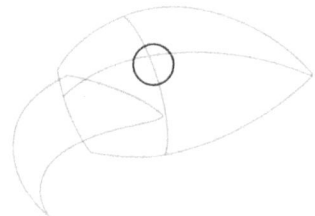

04

05

06

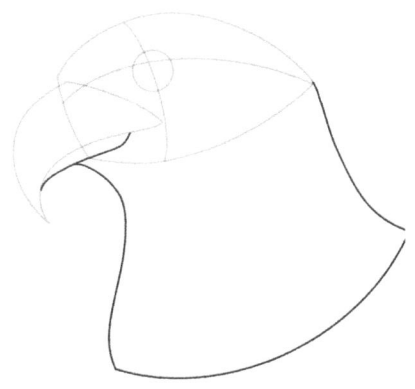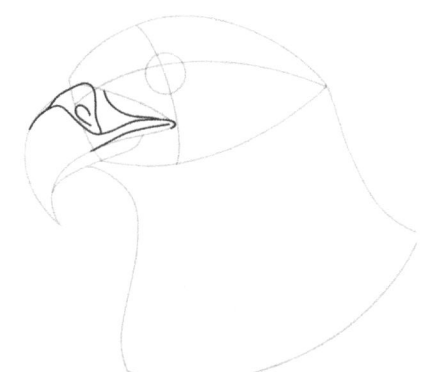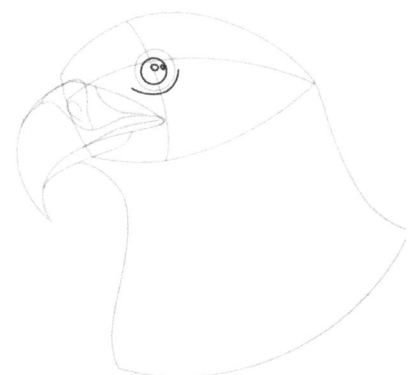

07

08

09

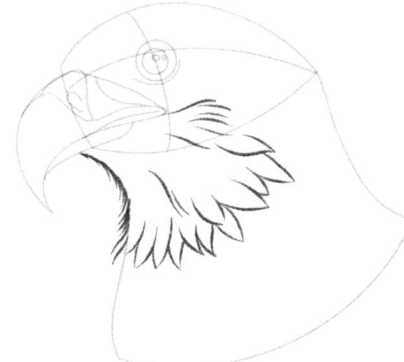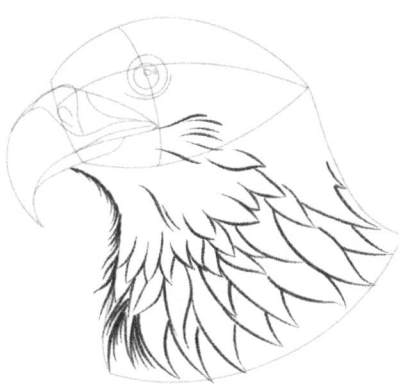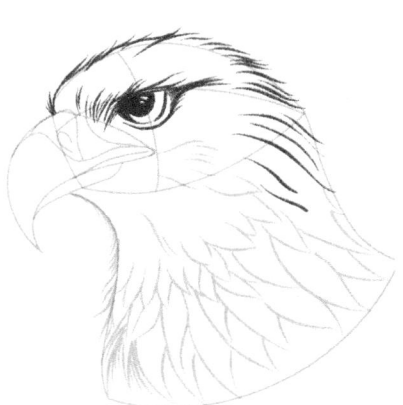

10

11

12

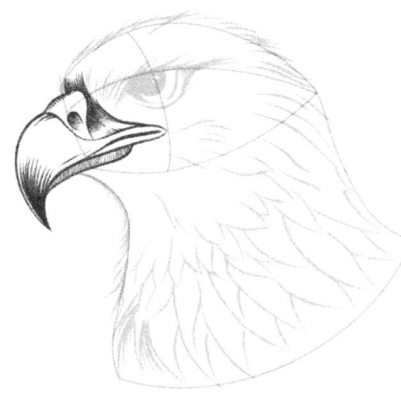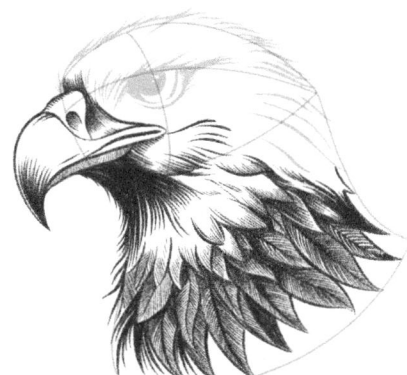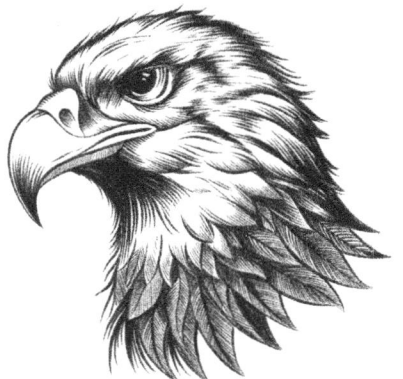

ELEPHANT

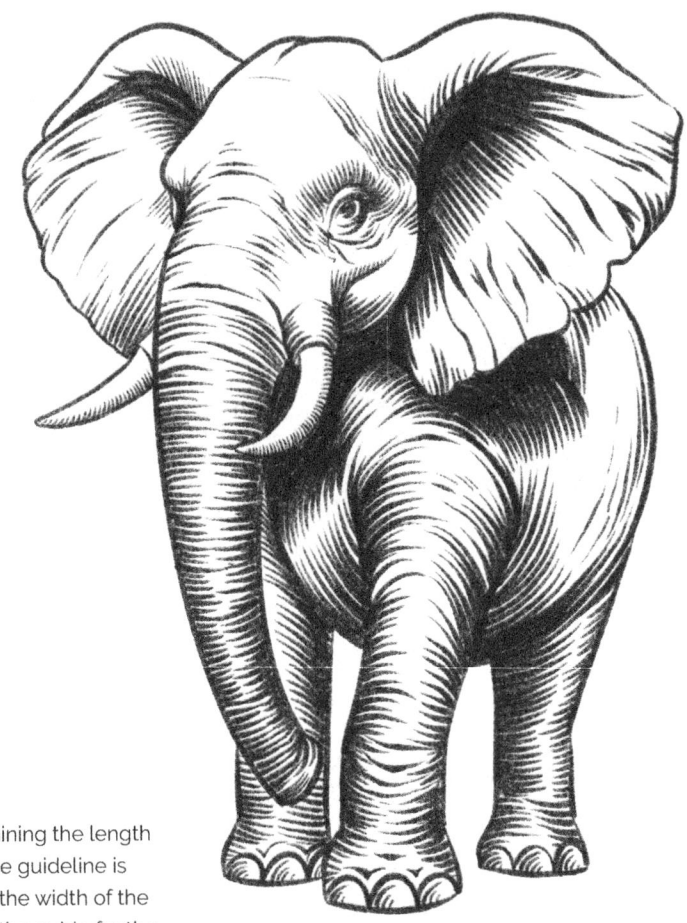

Pro Tip:
In step 02, when determining the length of the trunk, note that the guideline is approximately 1.5 times the width of the oval you have drawn as the guide for the elephant's head.

01

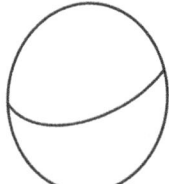

02

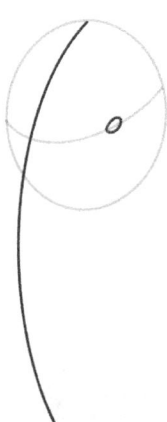

03

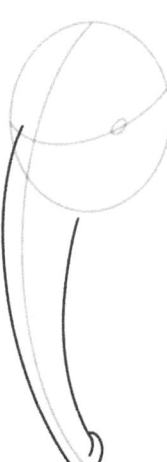

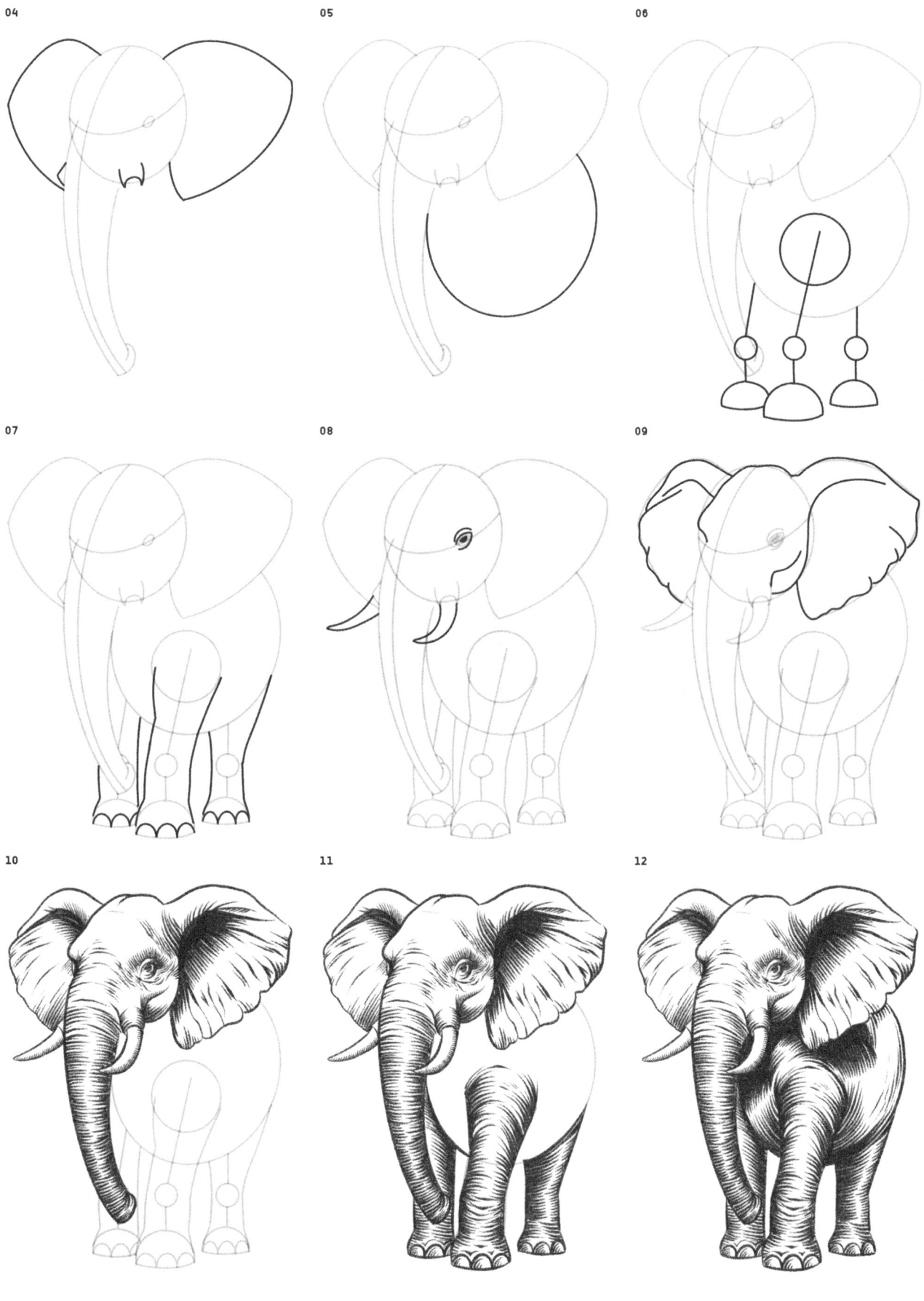

FOX

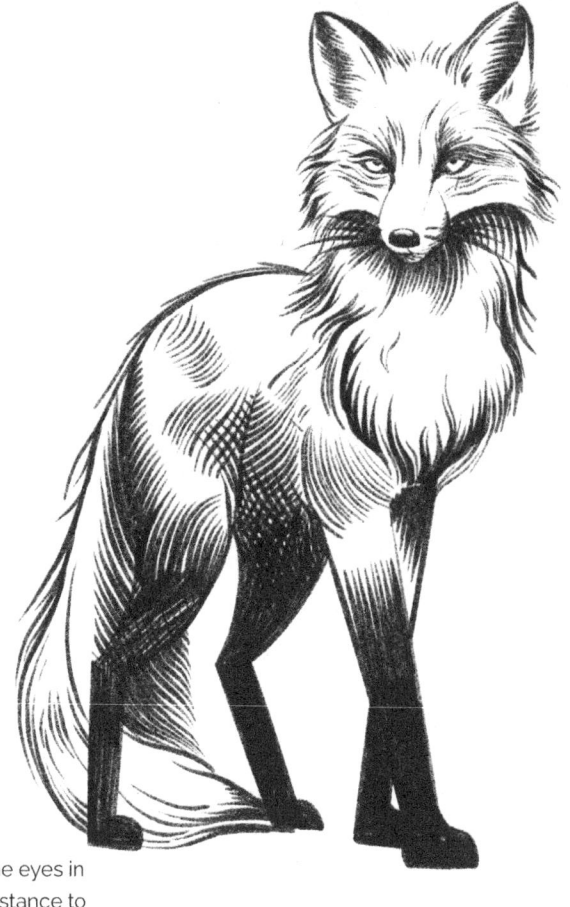

Pro Tip:
In step 02, note the spacing of the eyes in relation to the semi circle. The distance to the left edge should be slightly less than that of the right to account for the tilt of the head.

01

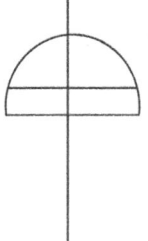

02

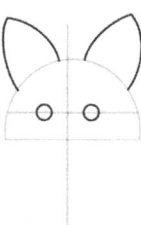

03

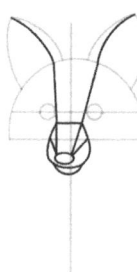

04

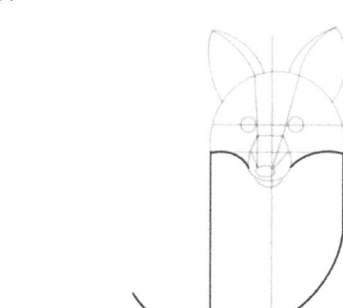

05

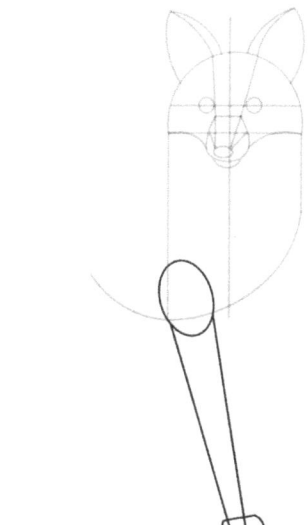

06

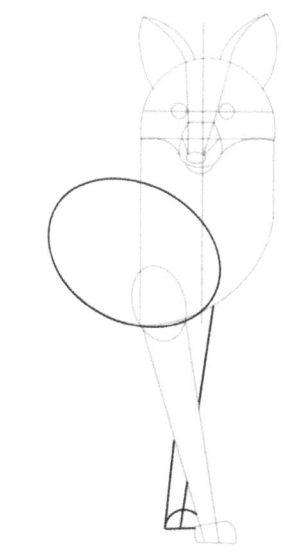

07

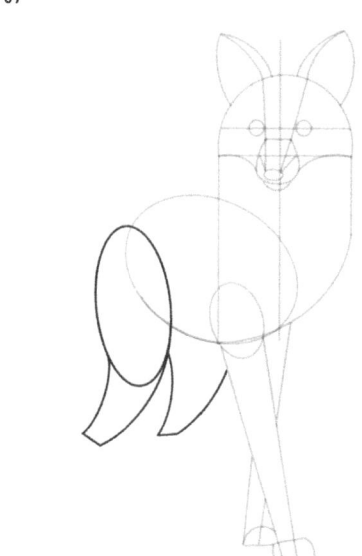

08

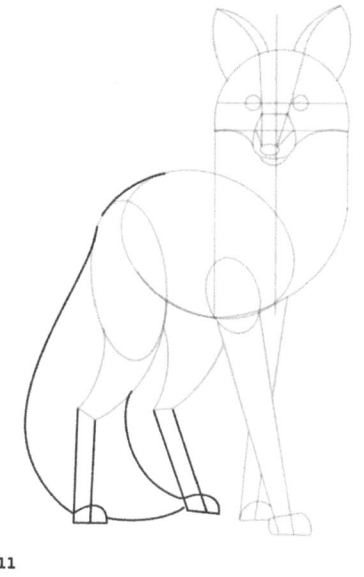

09

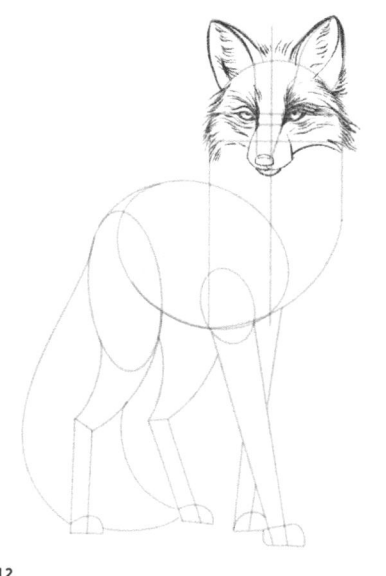

10

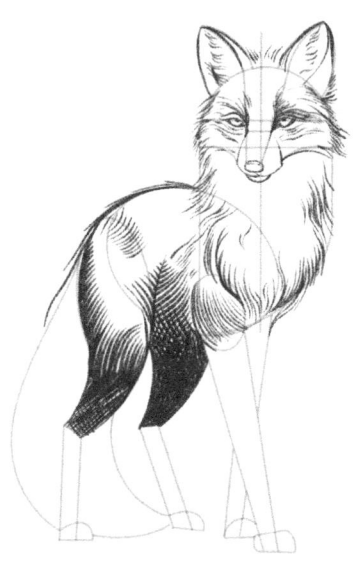

11

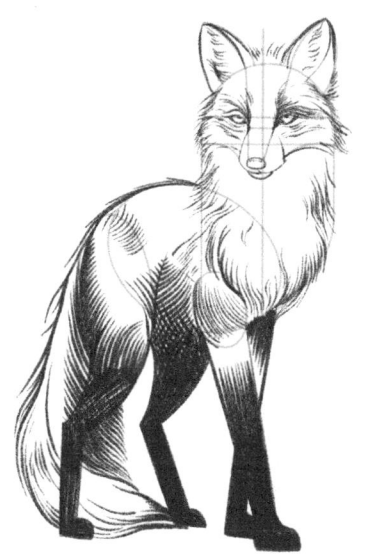

12

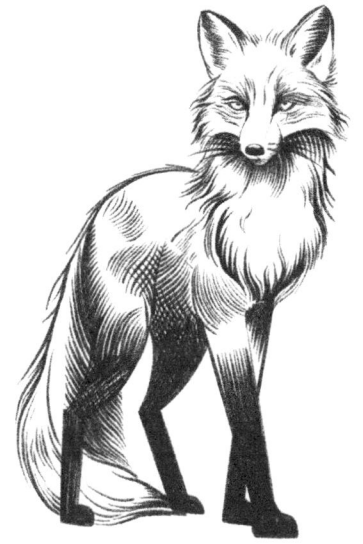

FROG

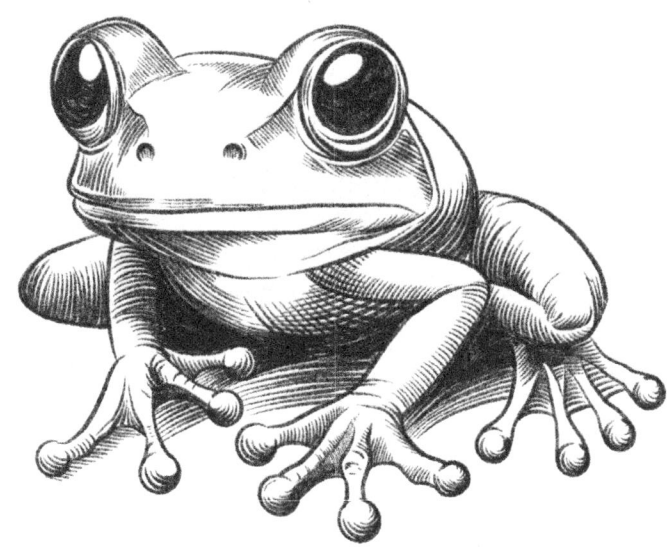

Pro Tip:
Once you have completed drawing the frog, sketch in some shadow under the body. It will provide a contrast that will help define the frog's form and make it look more natural.

01

02

03

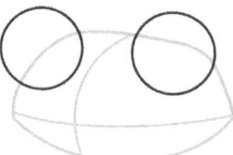

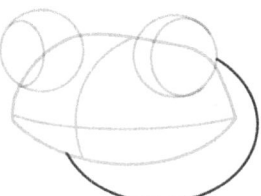

04

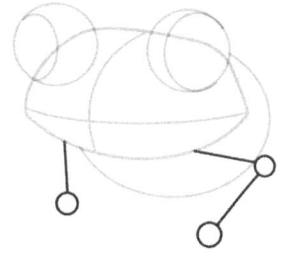

05

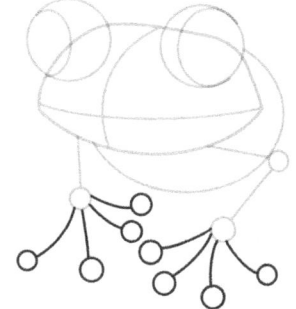

06

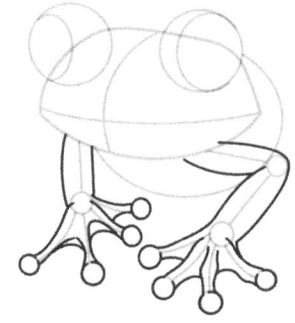

07

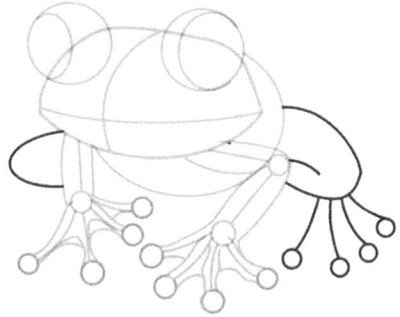

08

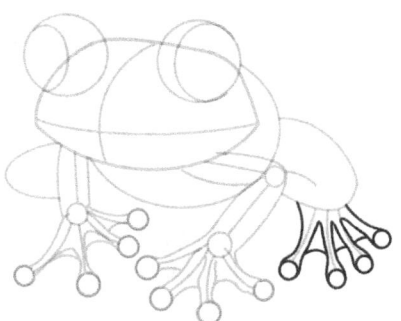

09

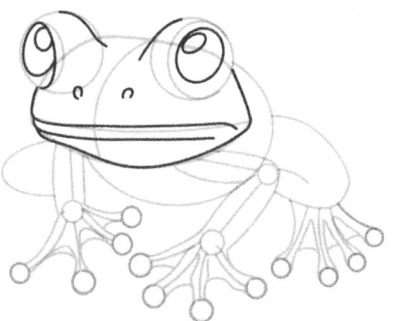

10

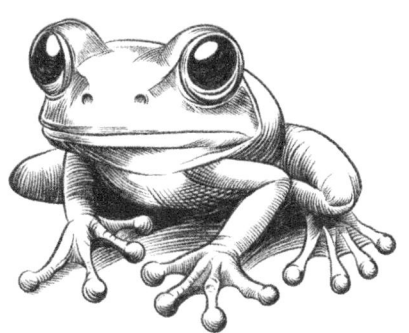

GIRAFFE

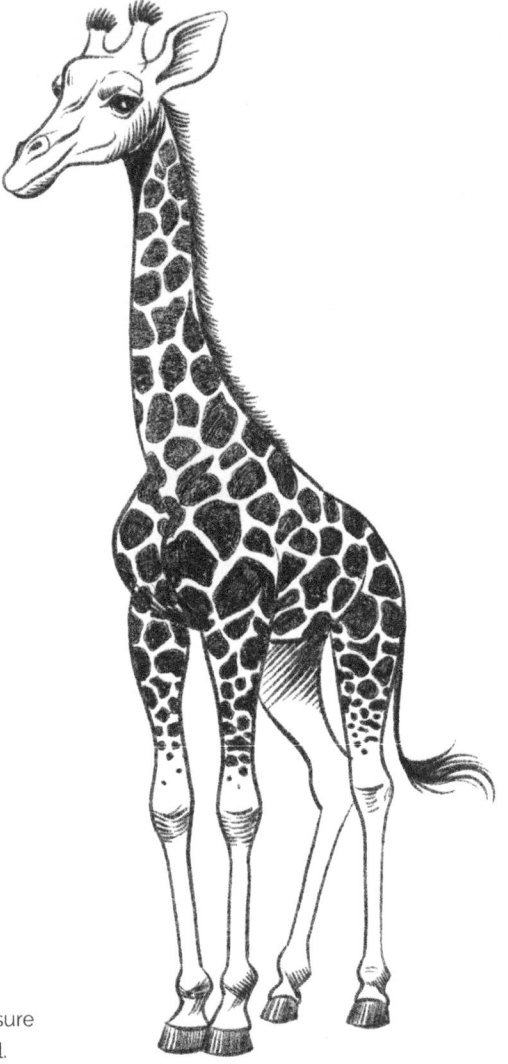

Pro Tip:
When drawing the legs of the giraffe, note that they are approximately the same size as the neck. This can be a helpful reference when working to ensure the proportions remain looking natural.

01

02

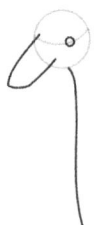

03

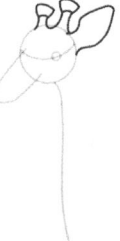

VOLUME.1　　　　　　　　　　　　　　　　　　　　　A STEP-BY-STEP GUIDE　　44

04
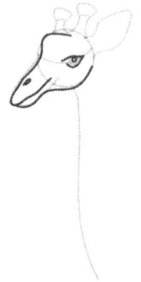

05
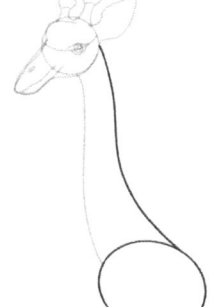

06
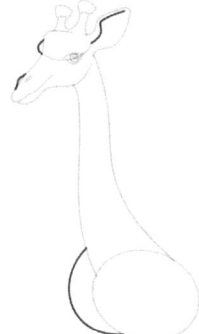

07
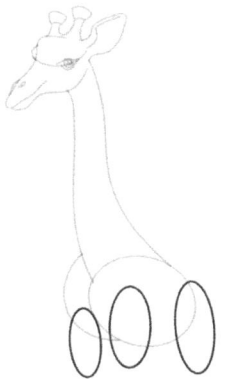

08
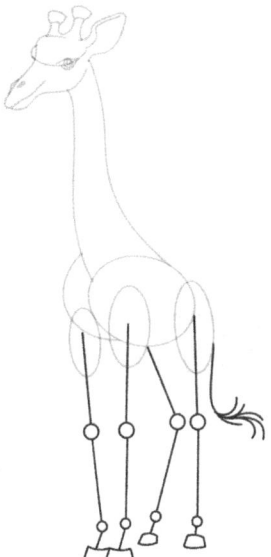

09
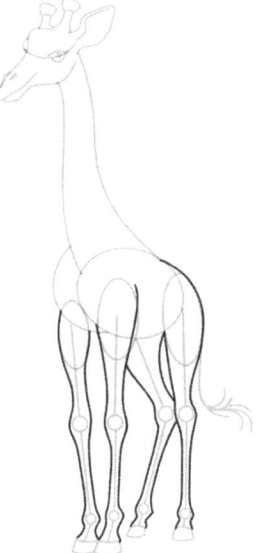

10
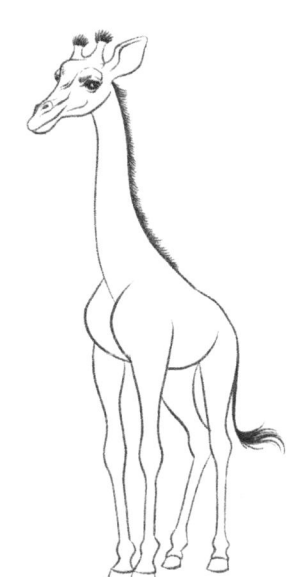

11
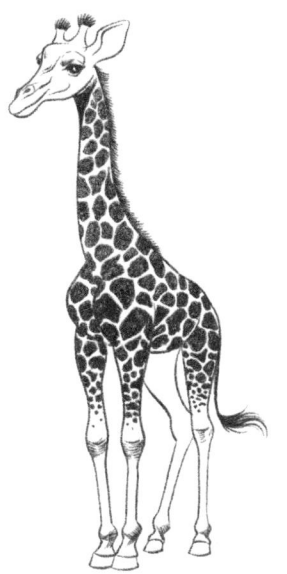

12
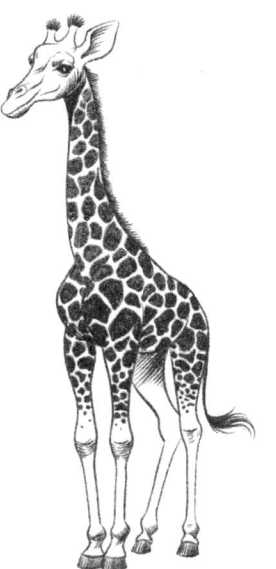

HOW TO DRAW ANIMALS

VAULTEDITIONS.COM

HORSE

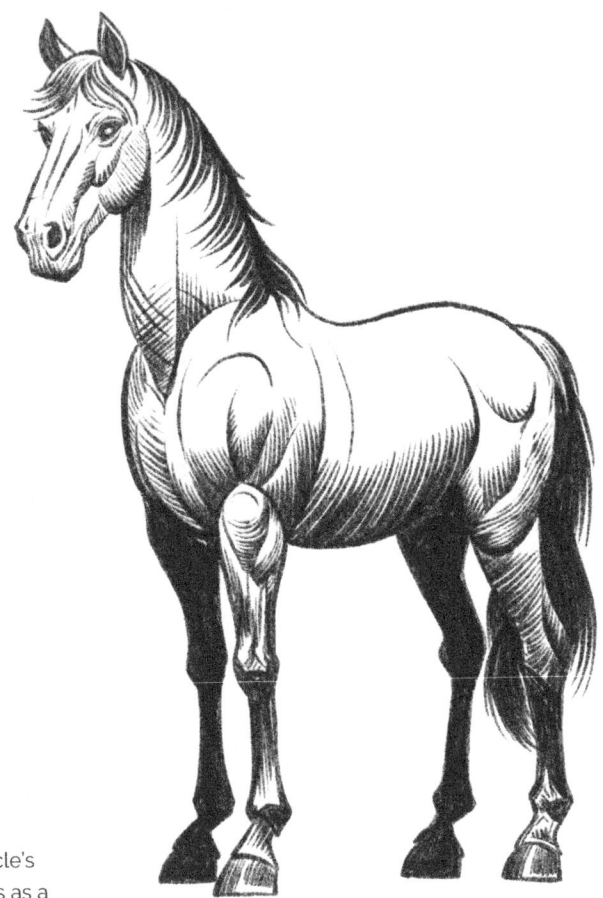

Pro Tip:
In step 2, draw the eye in the circle's centre first. You can then use this as a reference point for drawing the additional lines shown in this step.

01

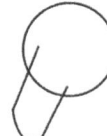

02

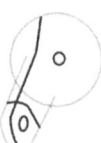

03

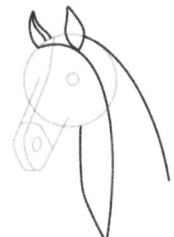

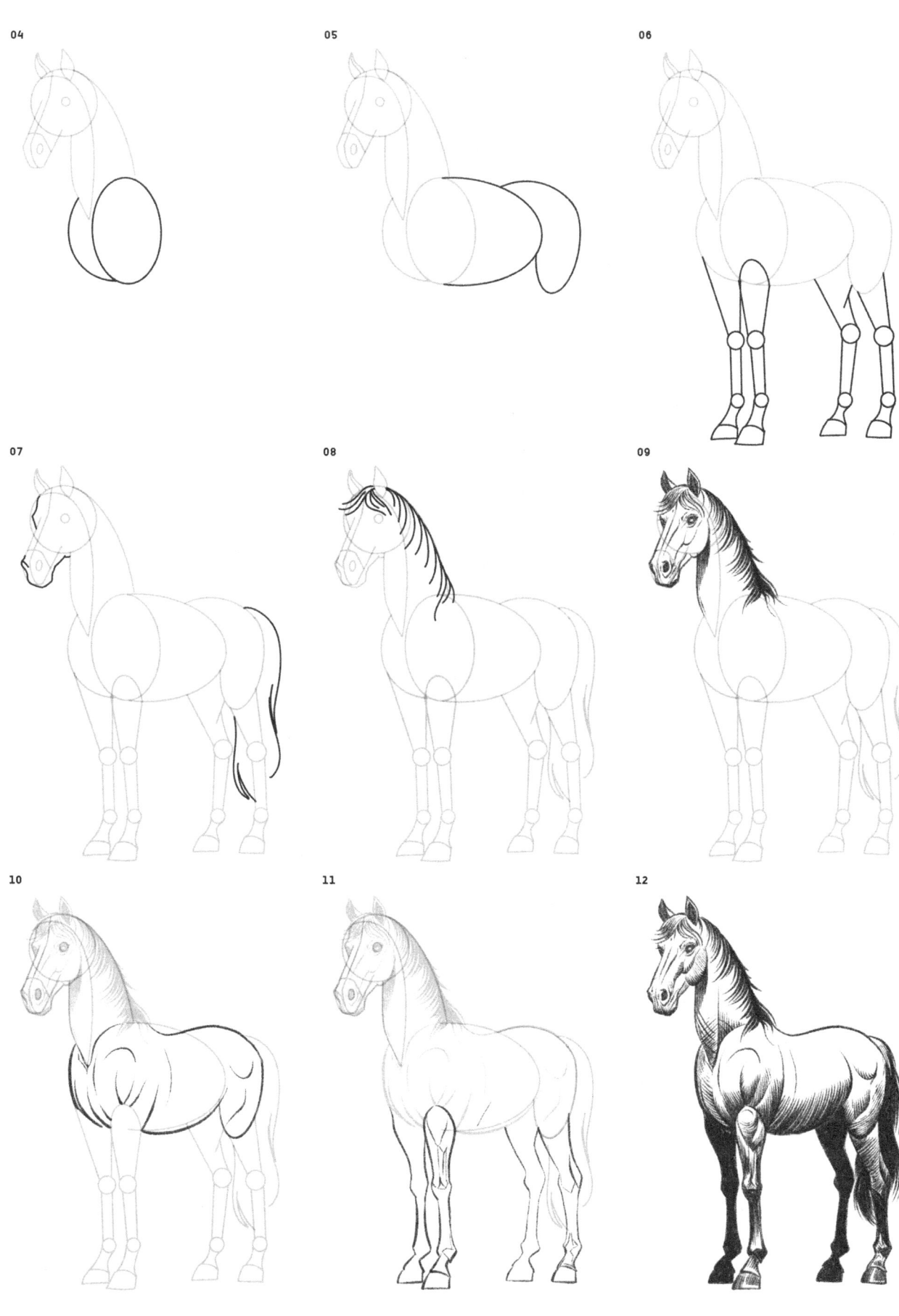

HORSE

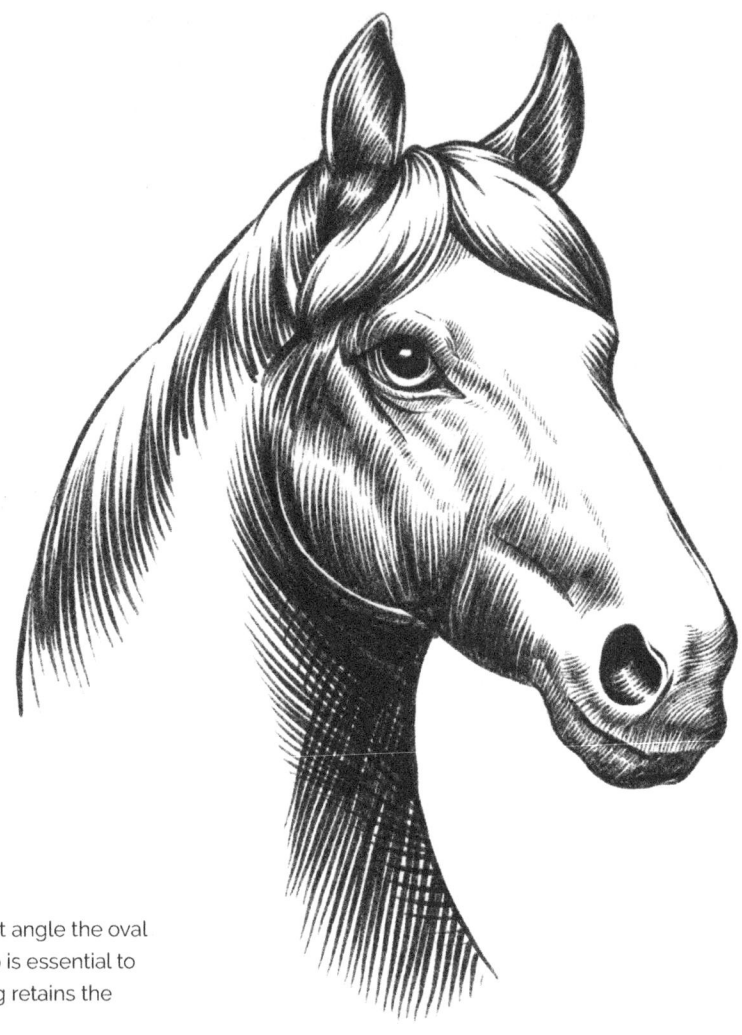

Pro Tip:
In step 01, note the slight angle the oval is on. Following this step is essential to ensure that your drawing retains the correct proportions.

01

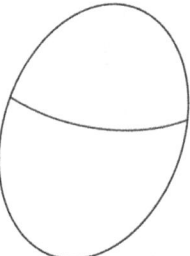

02

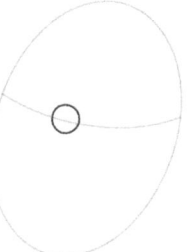

03

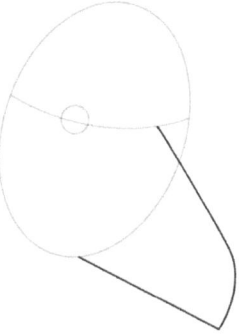

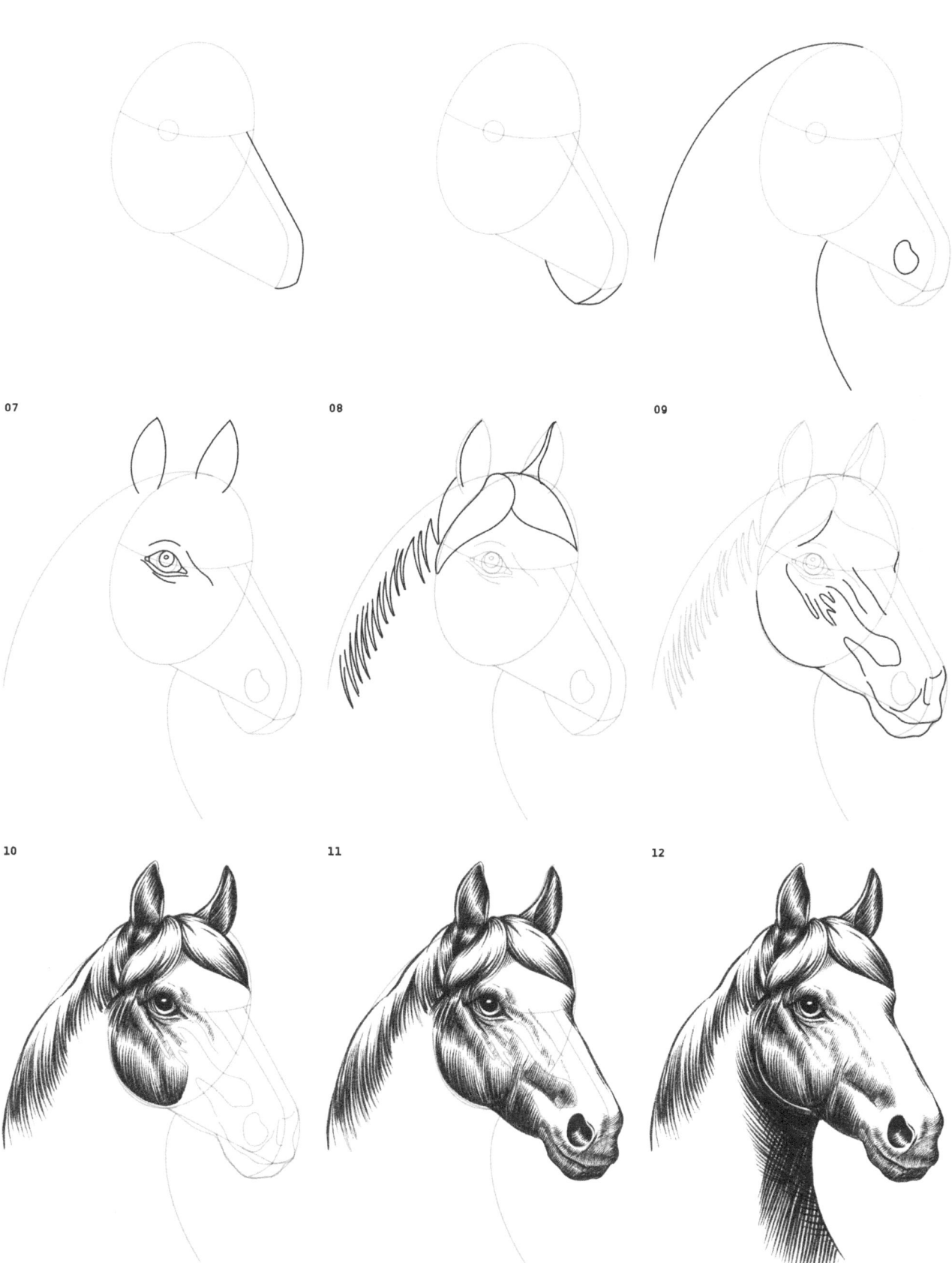

KANGAROO

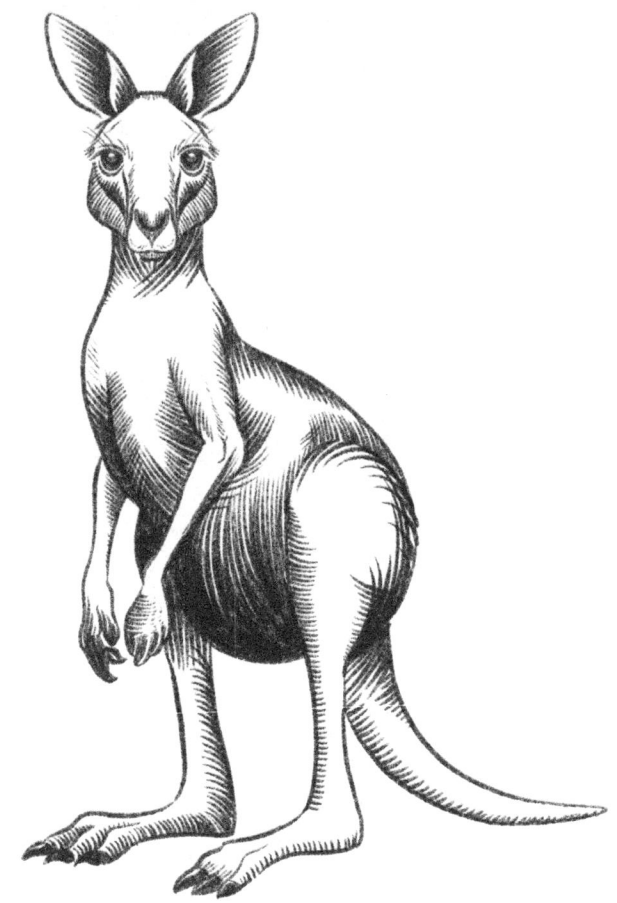

Pro Tip:
In step 03, when determining the placement of the oval that will form the upper leg, note that it should be positioned 3 times the height of the head down from the top and 2 times the head's width to the right.

01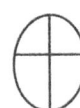

02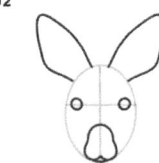

03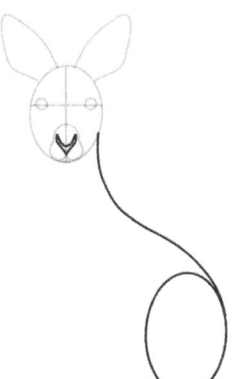

04
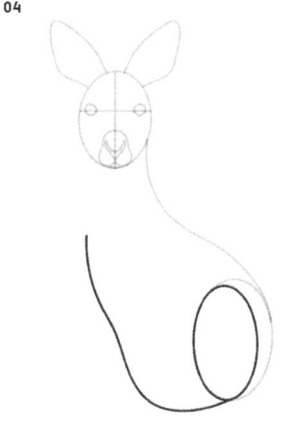

05
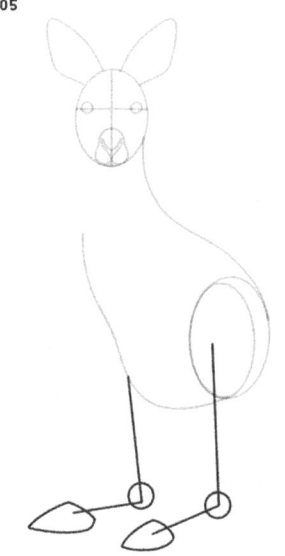

06
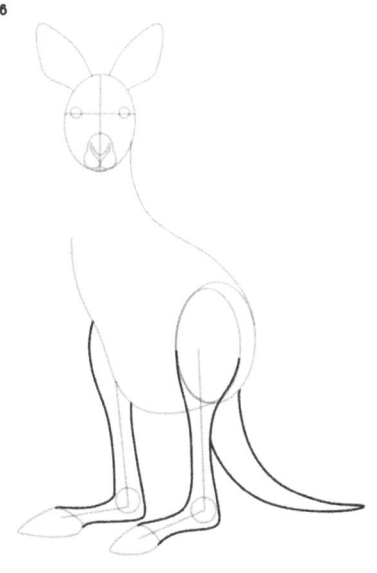

07
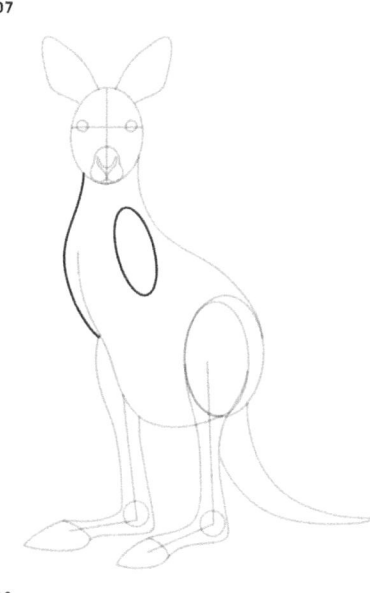

08
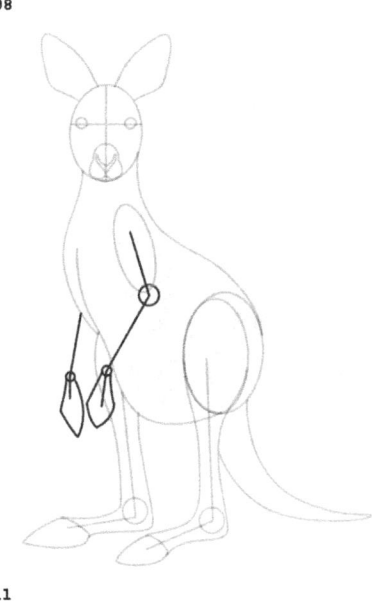

09
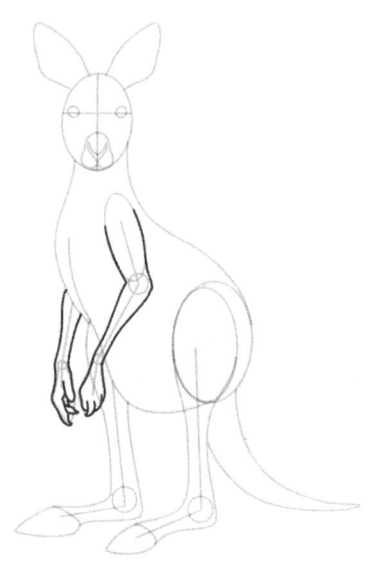

10
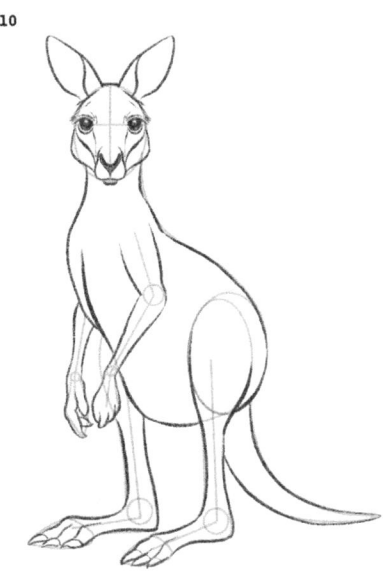

11
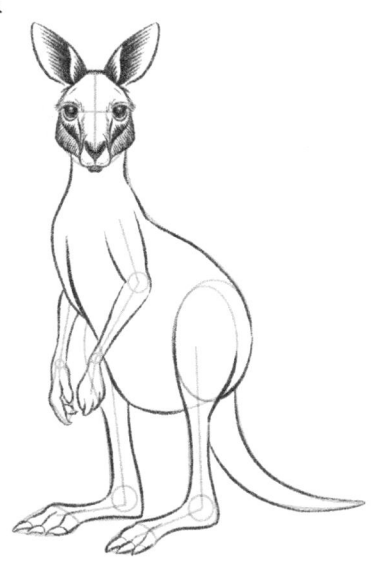

12
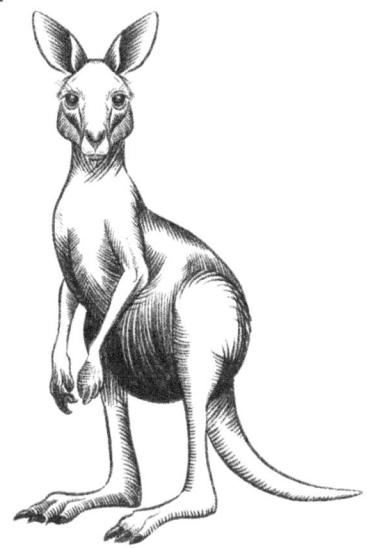

KOALA

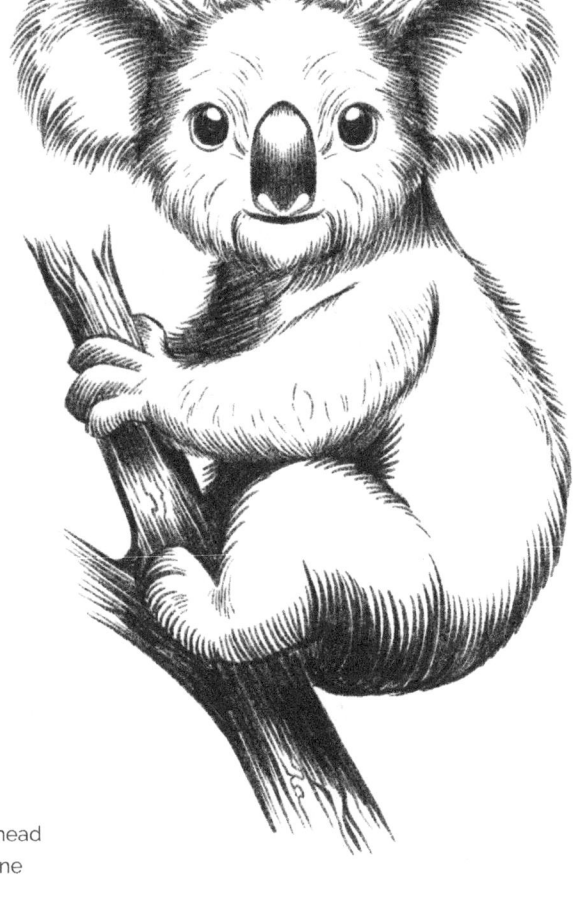

Pro Tip:
In step 03, when determining the placement of the oval that will form the upper leg, note that it should be positioned 2 times the height of the head down from the starting point of the line that connects them.

01

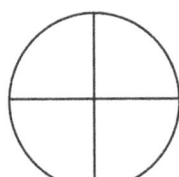

02

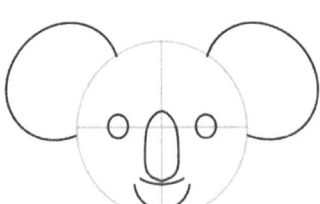

03

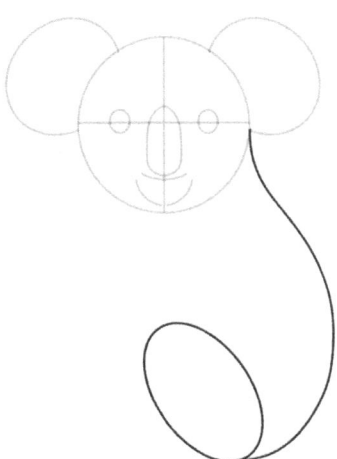

VOLUME.1　　　　　　　　　　　　　　　　　　　　A STEP-BY-STEP GUIDE　　52

04
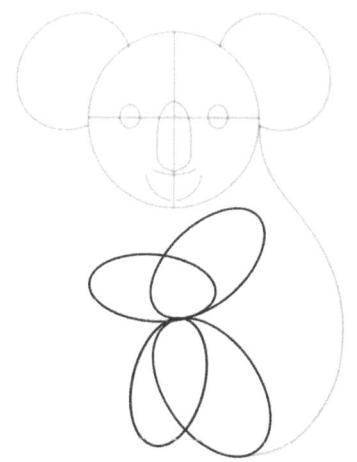

05
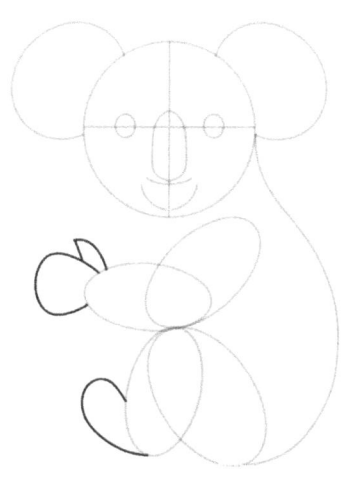

06
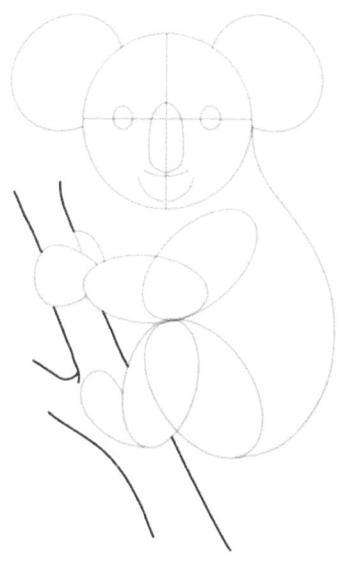

07
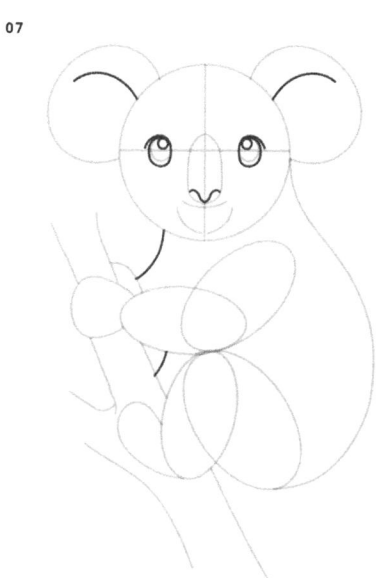

08
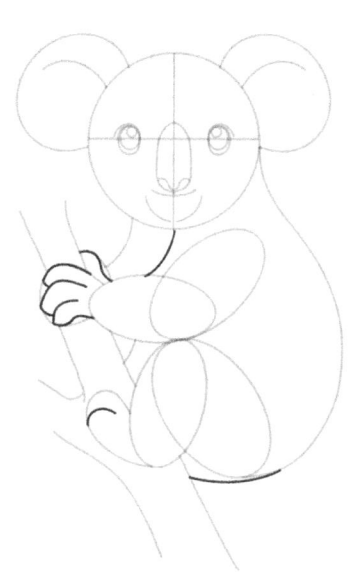

09
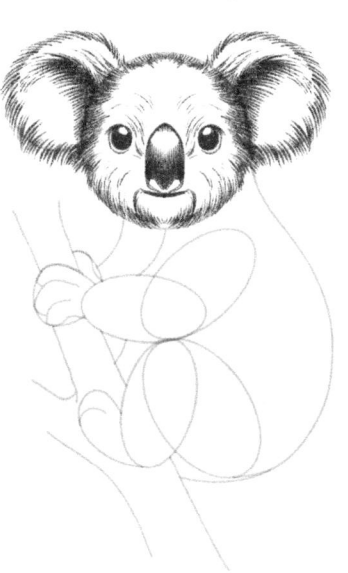

10
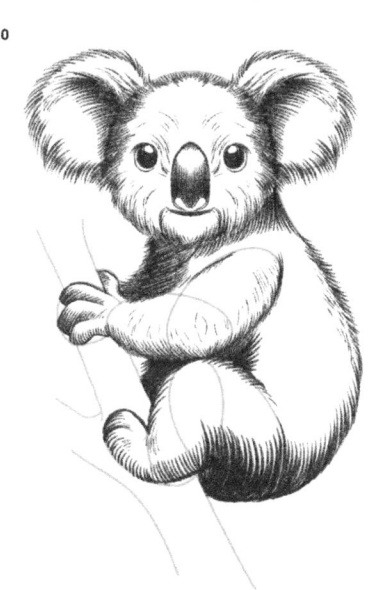

11
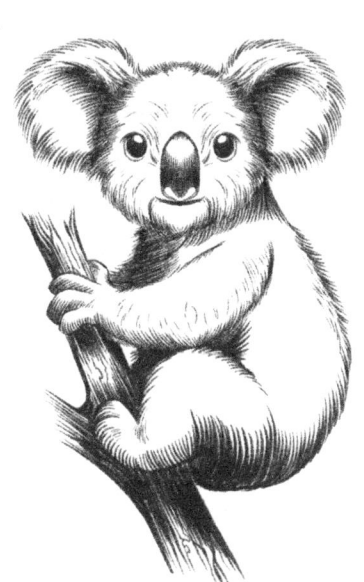

HOW TO DRAW ANIMALS

VAULTEDITIONS.COM

LIZARD

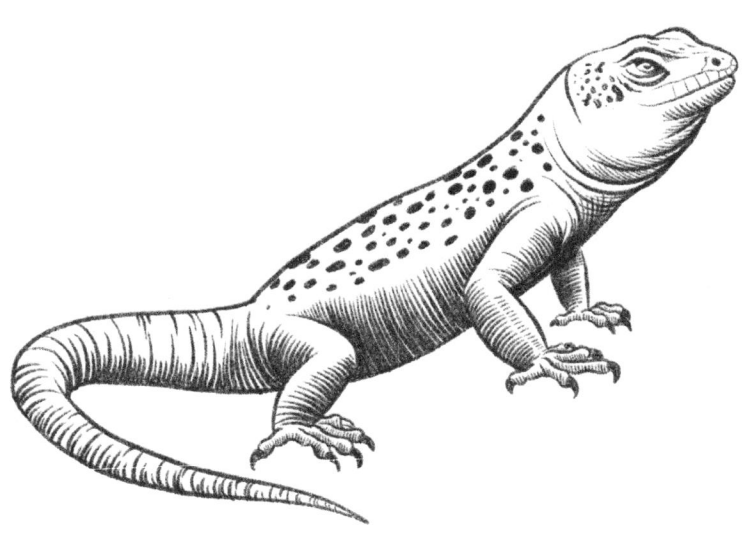

Pro Tip:
In step 04, Note that the upper leg is not centred directly within the midsection of the lizard's body but slightly lower. It is crucial to note this step to ensure the lizard looks anatomically accurate.

01

02

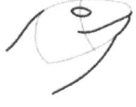

03

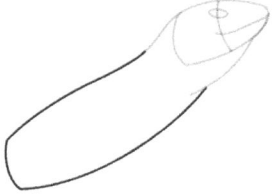

VOLUME.1   A STEP-BY-STEP GUIDE

04

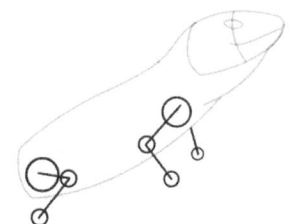

05

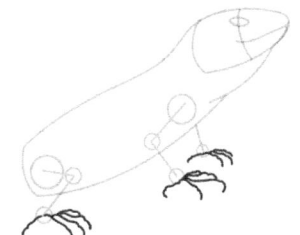

06

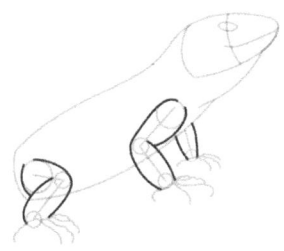

07

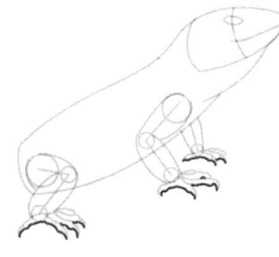

08

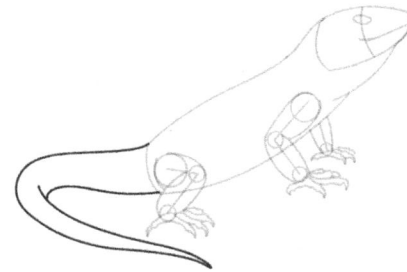

09

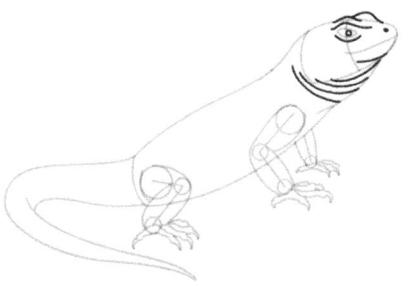

10

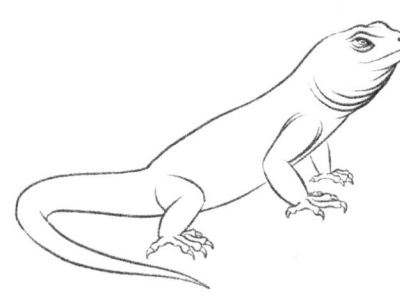

11

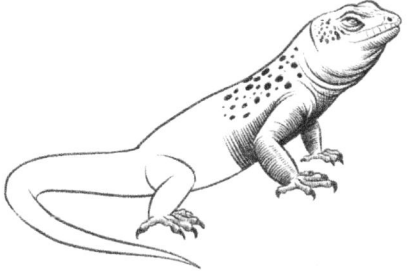

12

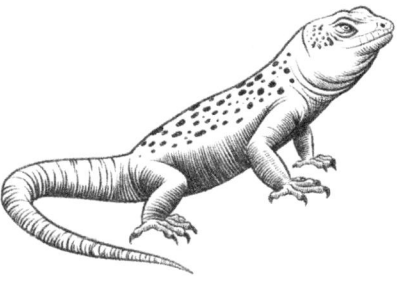

HOW TO DRAW ANIMALS

VAULTEDITIONS.COM

LLAMA

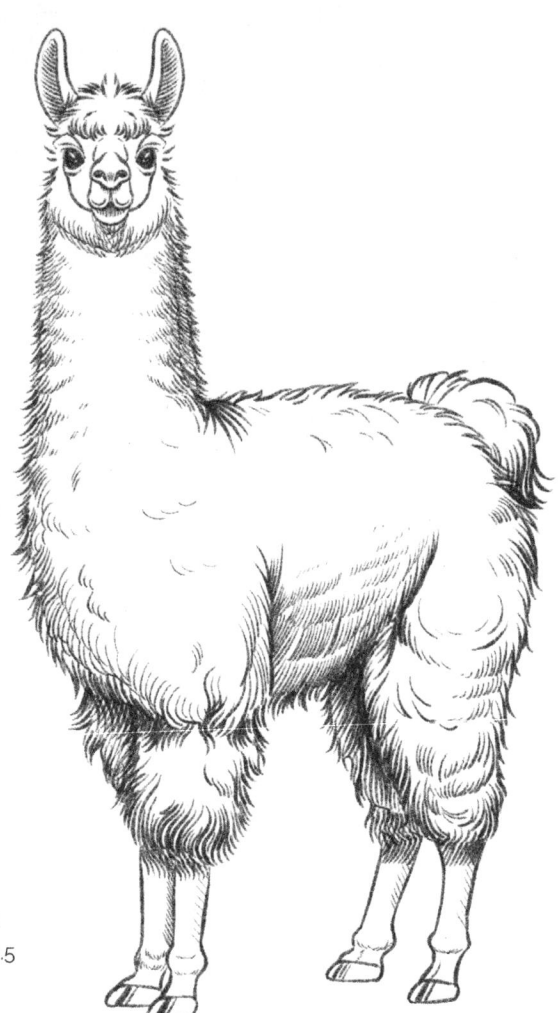

Pro Tip:
In step 01, the length of the line that descends from the oval should be 3.5 times the height of said oval.

01

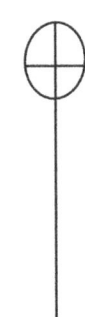

02

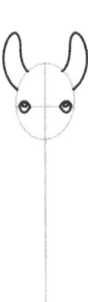

03

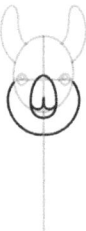

VOLUME.1 A STEP-BY-STEP GUIDE

04

05
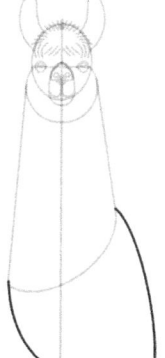

06
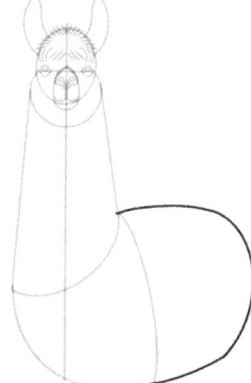

07
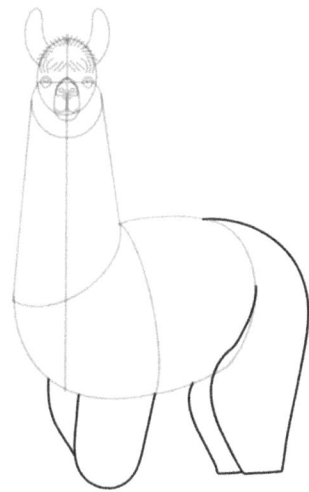

08
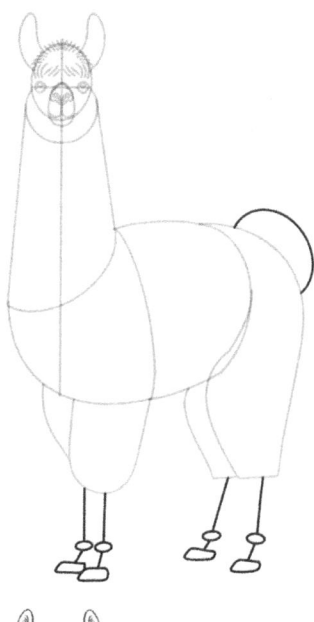

09
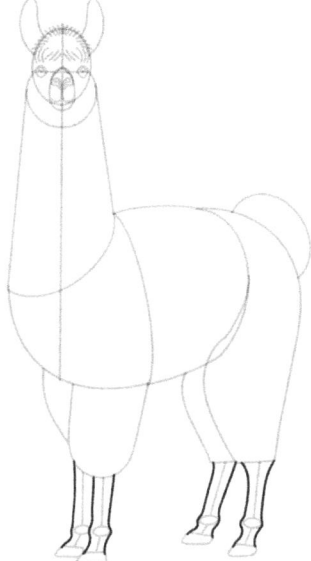

10
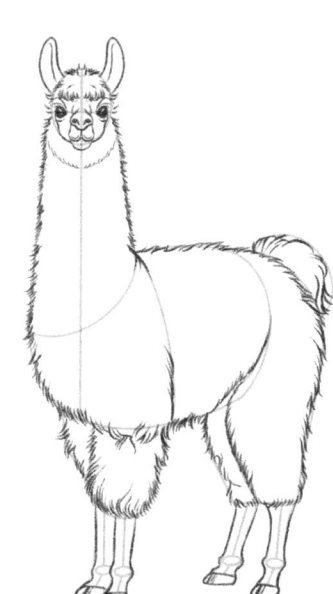

11
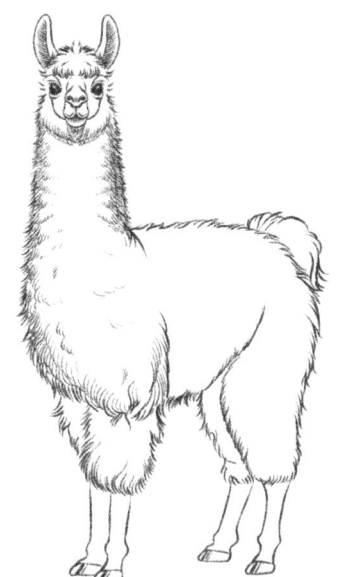

12
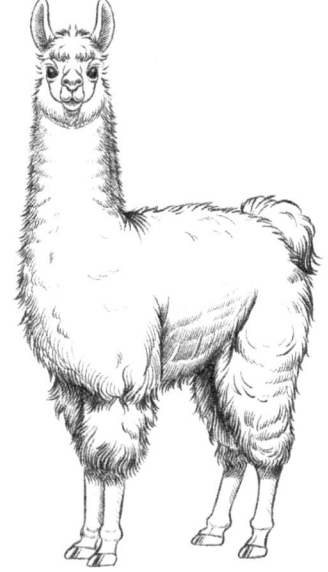

HOW TO DRAW ANIMALS

OCTOPUS

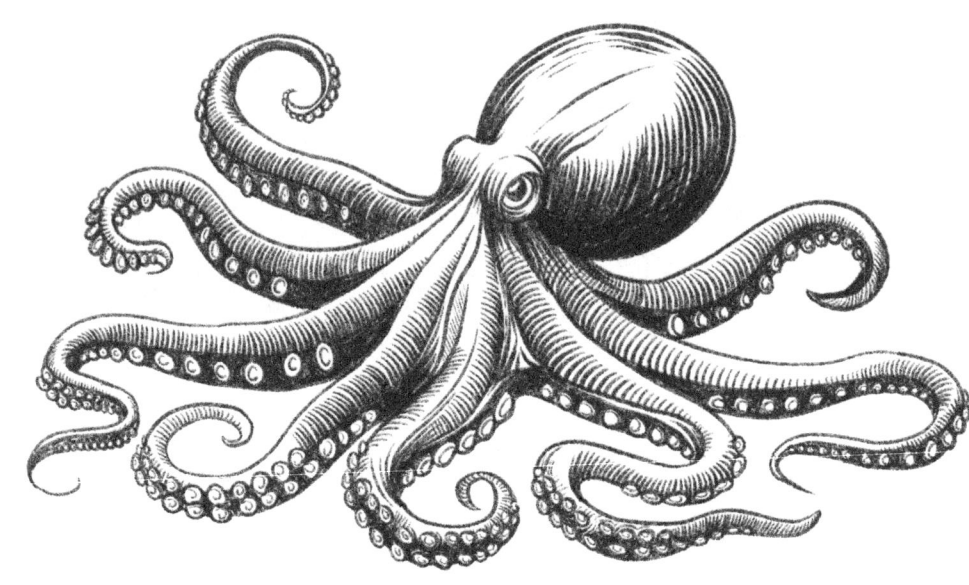

Pro Tip:

In step 02, when drawing the eyes, it can be helpful to imagine that you are drawing a cylinder with equal-sized faces that have not been connected. One could draw the cylinder and erase the connecting lines.

01

02

03

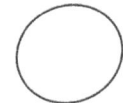

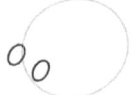

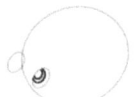

04

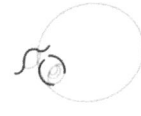

05

06

07

08

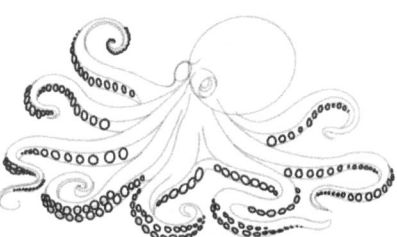

09

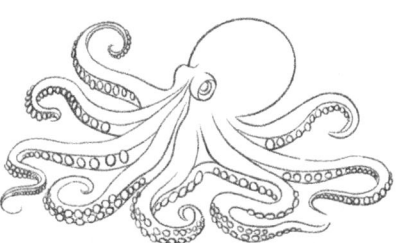

10

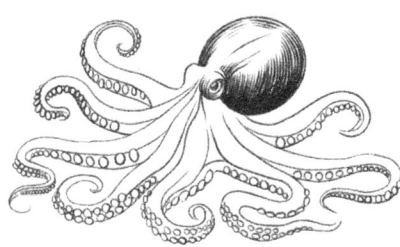

11

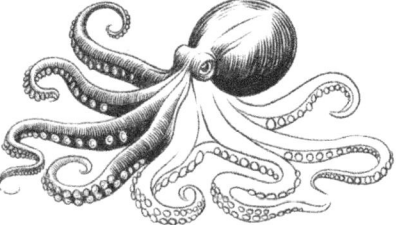

12

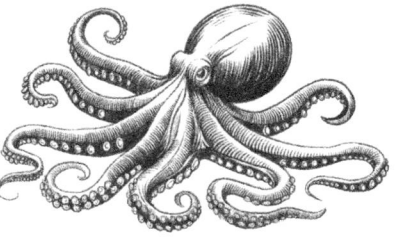

OWL

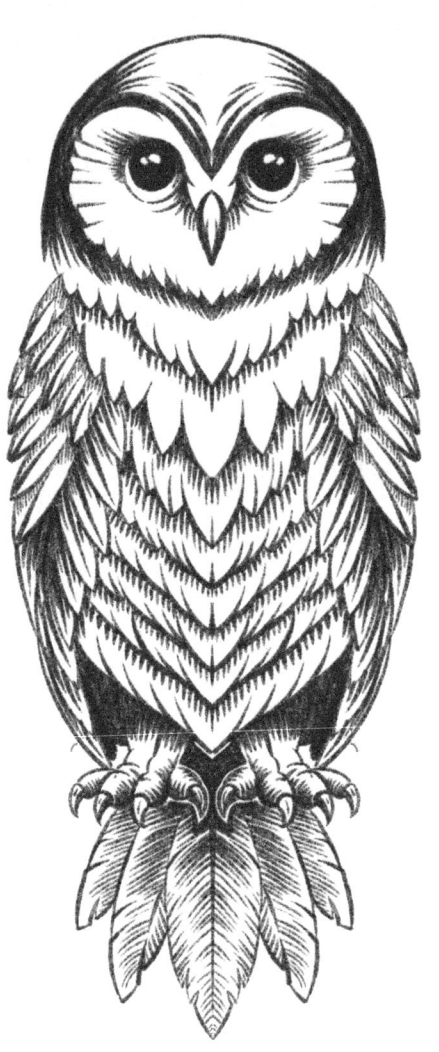

Pro Tip:
In step 01, the length of the line that descends from the oval shape that will make the head of the owl should be 2.5 times the height of said oval.

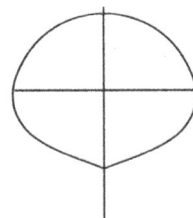

02
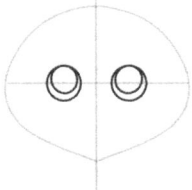

03
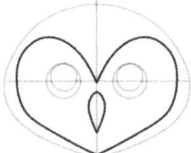

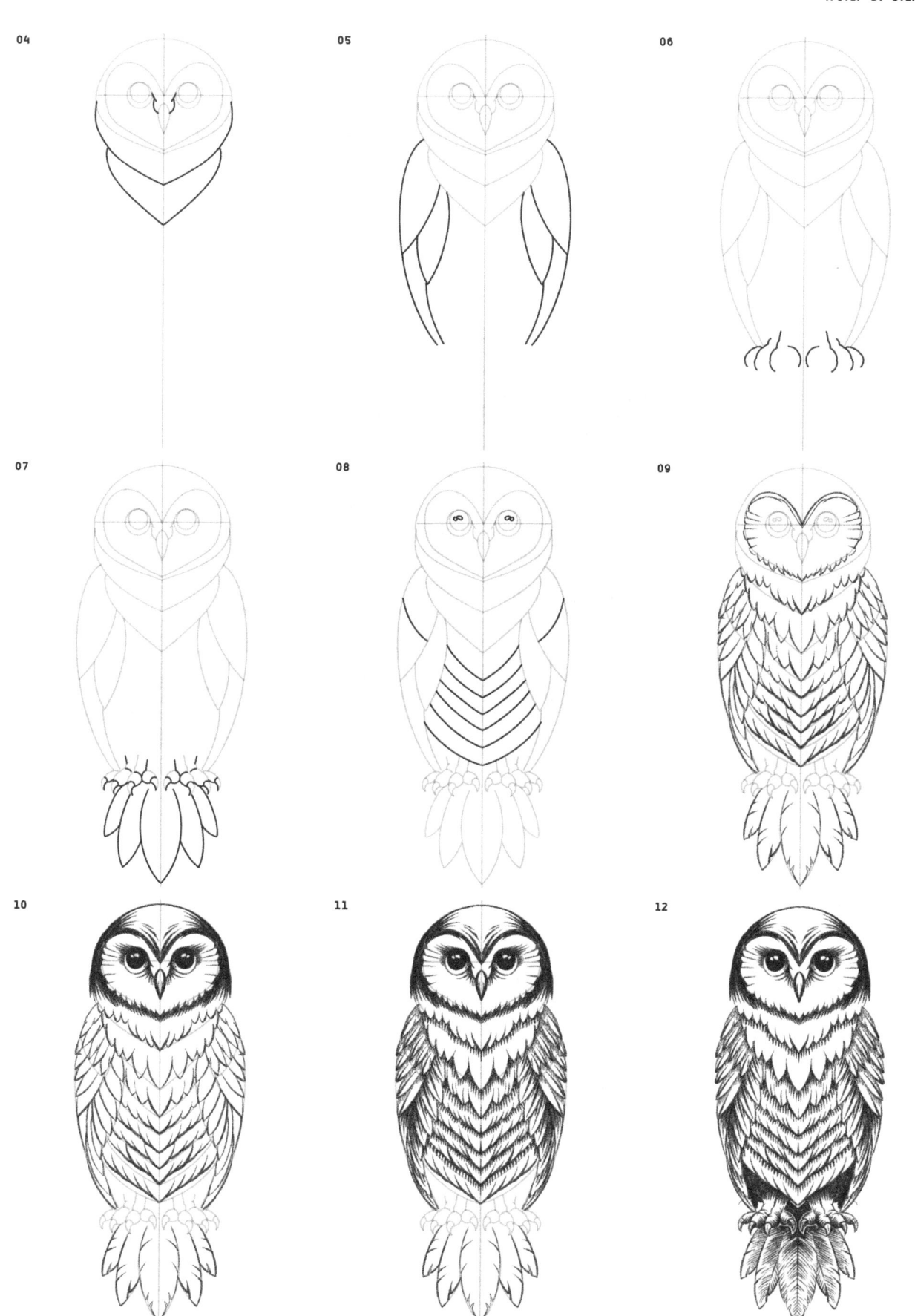

PANDA

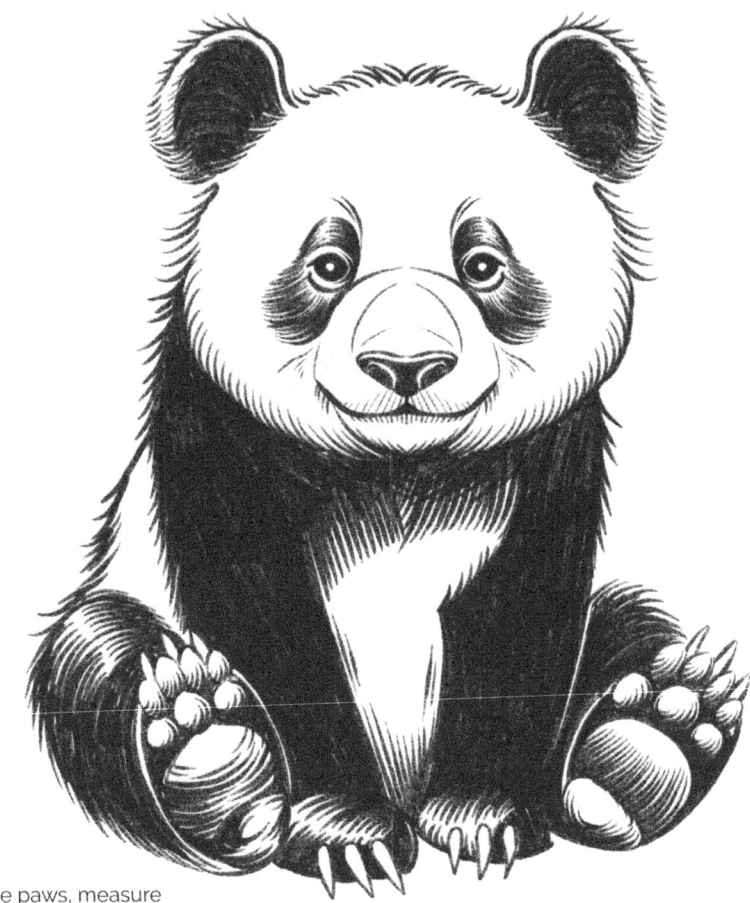

Pro Tip:
In step 04, to position the paws, measure the height of the head. From the base of the head, draw a guide down the length of the measurement you have taken. At the base of this guide is where the paws should be drawn.

01

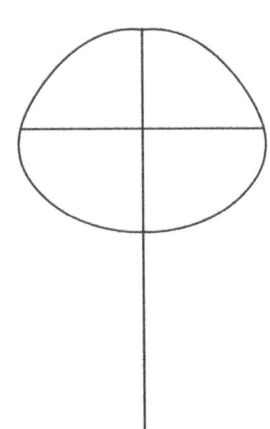

02

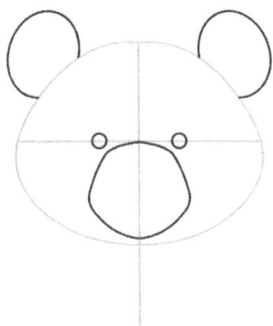

03

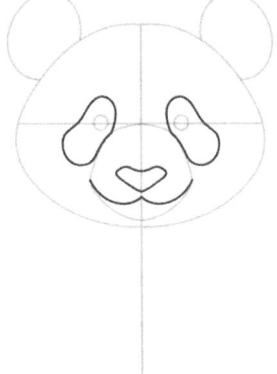

04

05

06

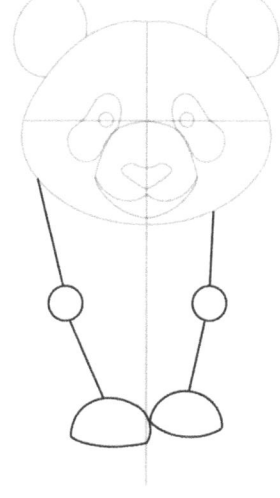
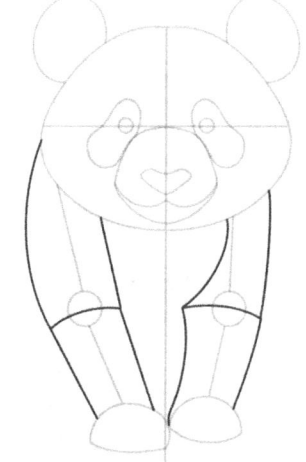
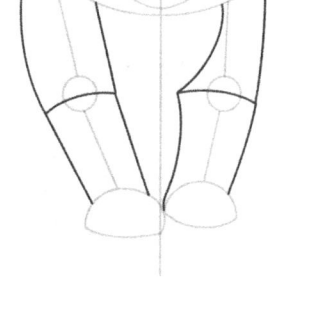

07

08

09

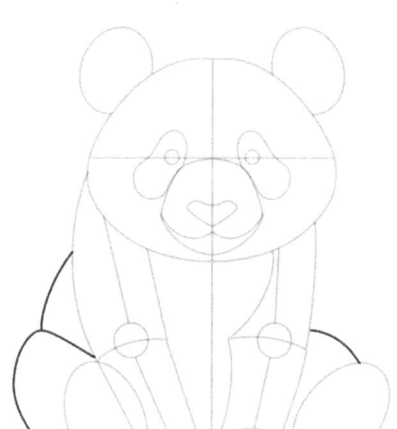
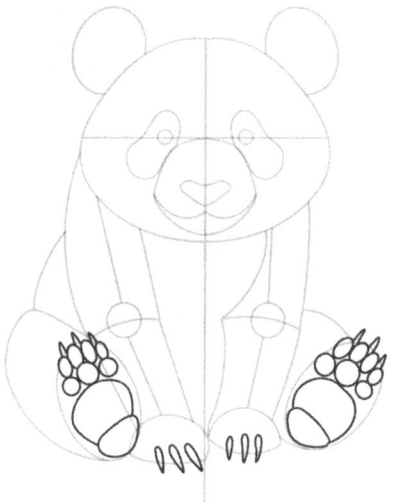
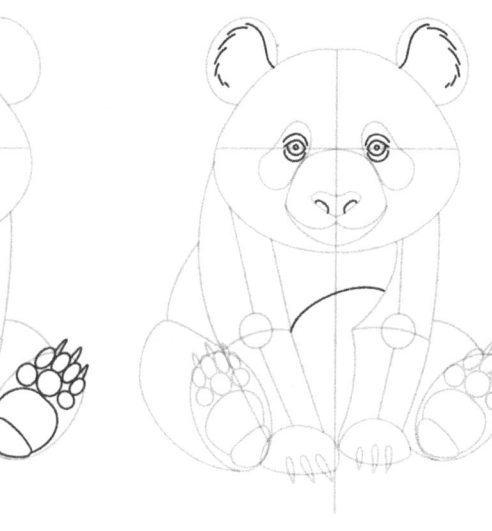

10

11

12

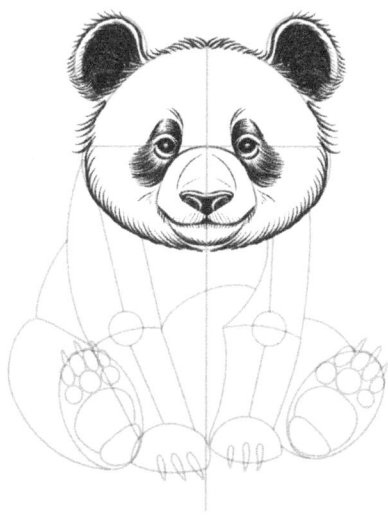
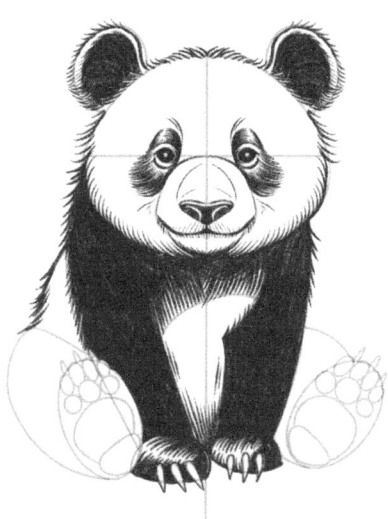
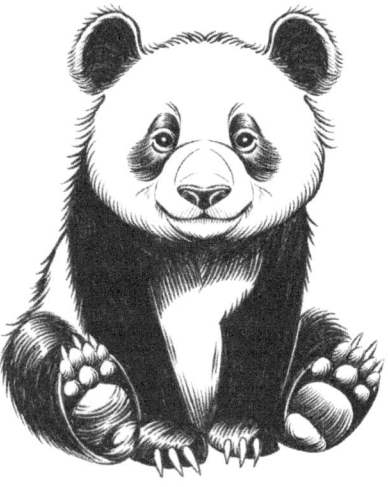

PENGUIN

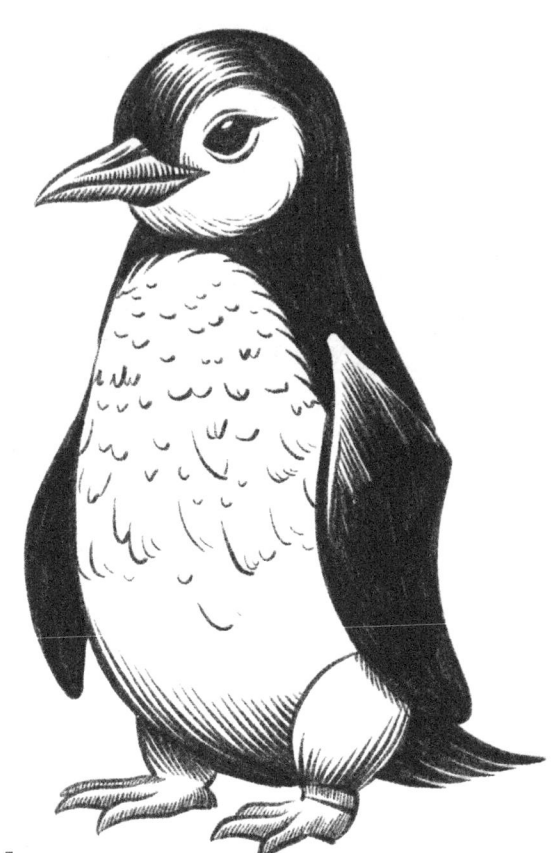

Pro Tip:
In step 03, the length of the line that descends from the circle should be 2.5 times the height of said circle.

01

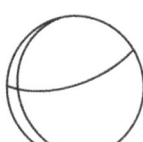

02

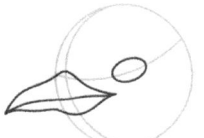

03

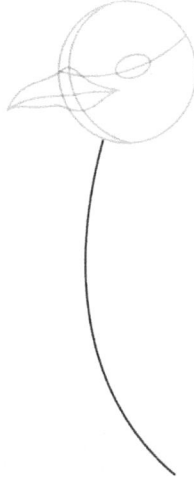

VOLUME.1 A STEP-BY-STEP GUIDE

04
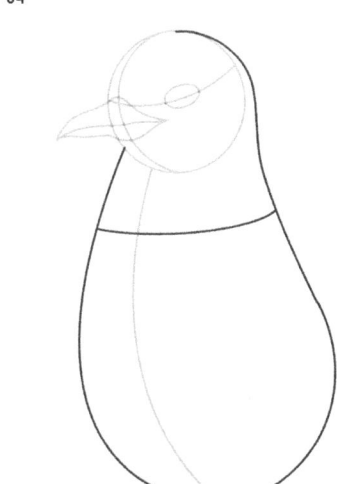

05
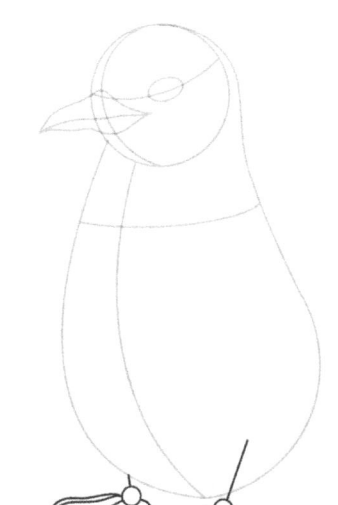

06
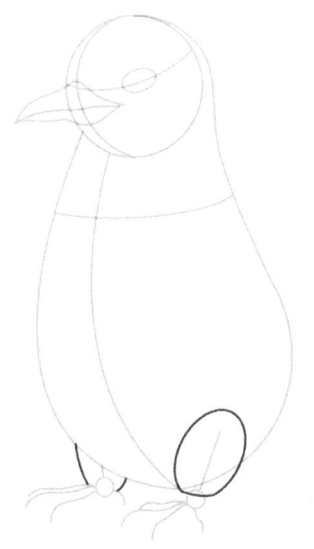

07
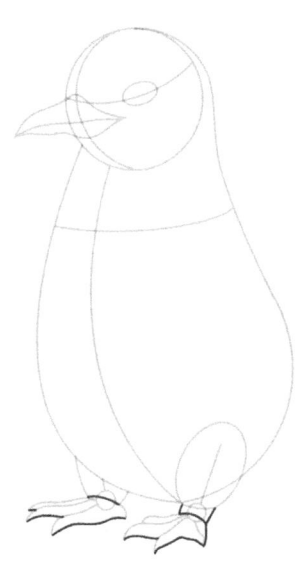

08
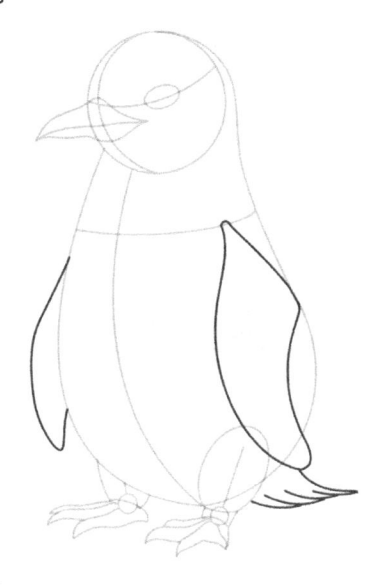

09
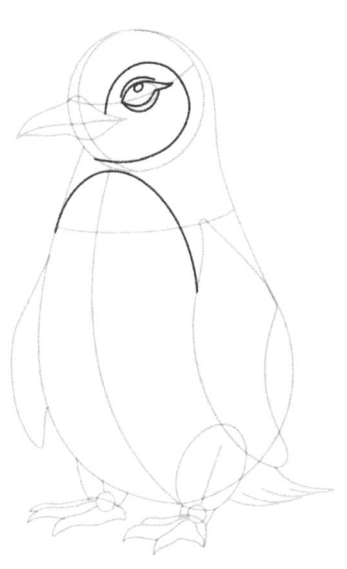

10
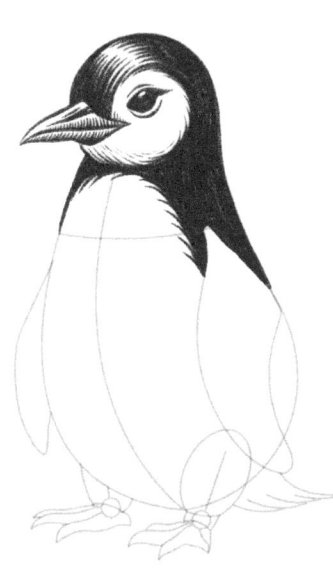

11
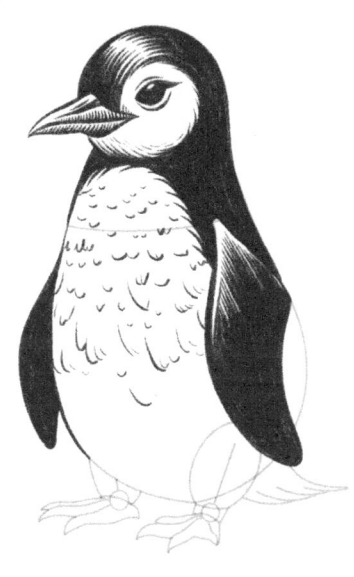

12
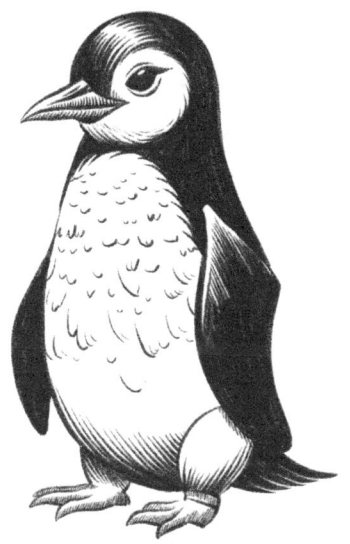

HOW TO DRAW ANIMALS

VAULTEDITIONS.COM

VOLUME.1   A STEP-BY-STEP GUIDE

SNAKE

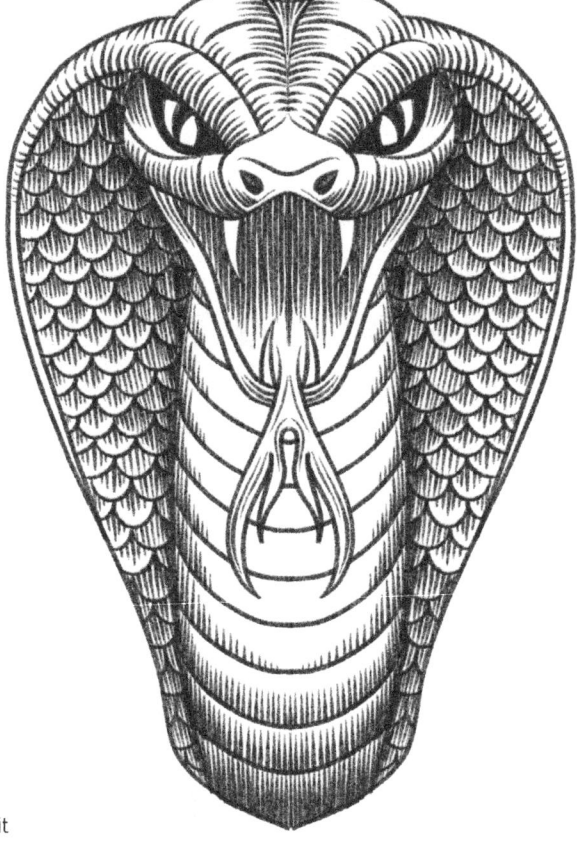

Pro Tip:
In step 11, when drawing the scale pattern, one line of scales should fit precisely between the guidelines, while the proceeding line of scales below should intersect the line directly in the middle of the scale, and so on.

01

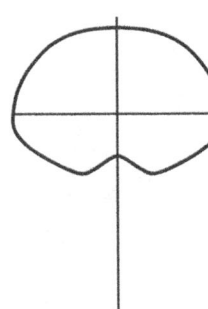

02

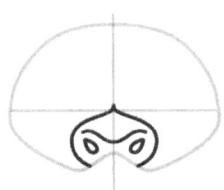

03

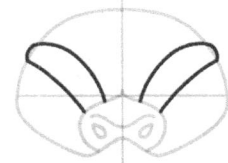

VAULTEDITIONS.COM

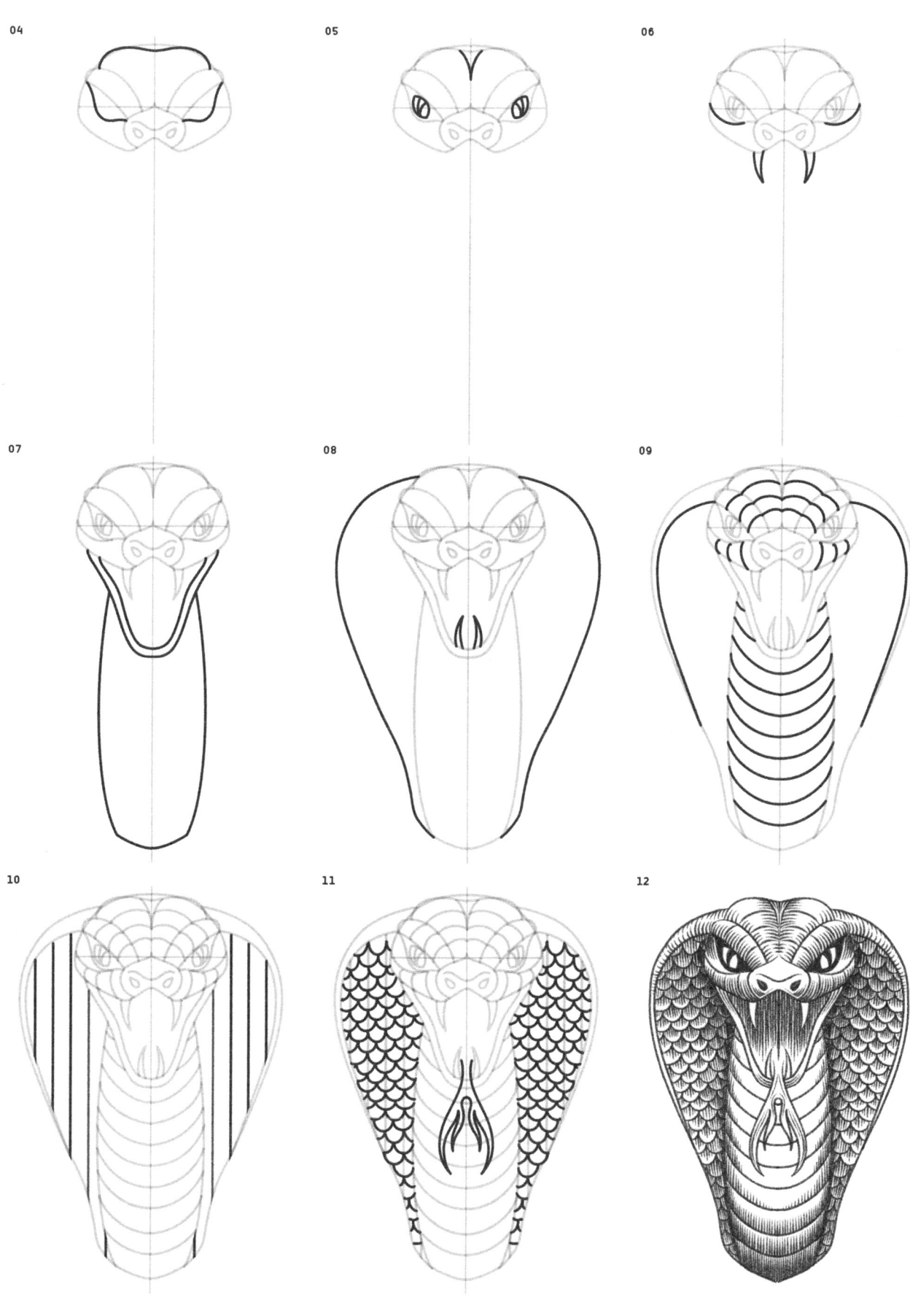

STAG

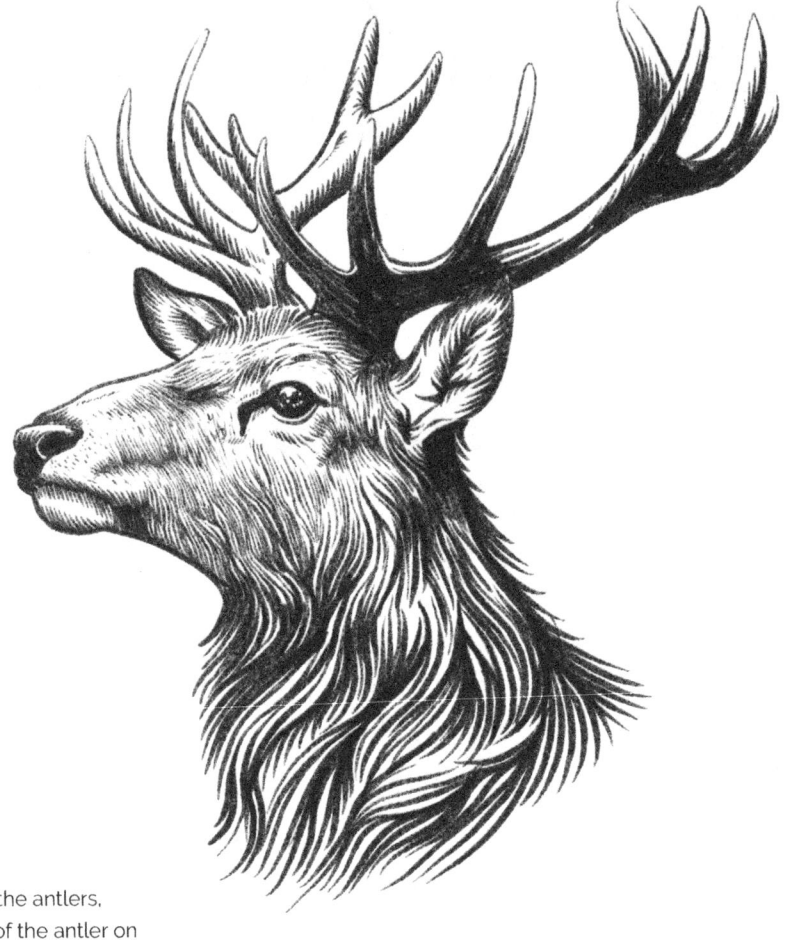

Pro Tip:
In step 03, when drawing the antlers, ensure that the top point of the antler on the right side is slightly higher than on the left. Following this step will provide a natural-looking perspective.

01

02

03

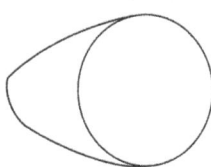
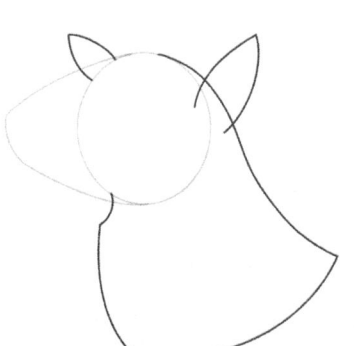
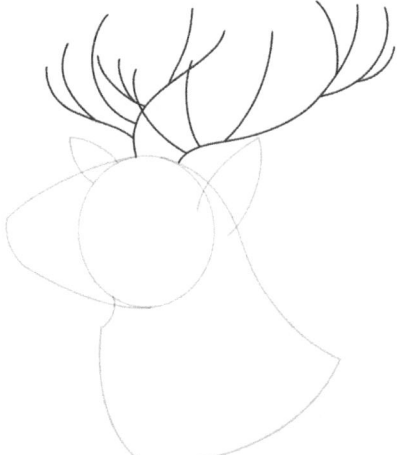

04

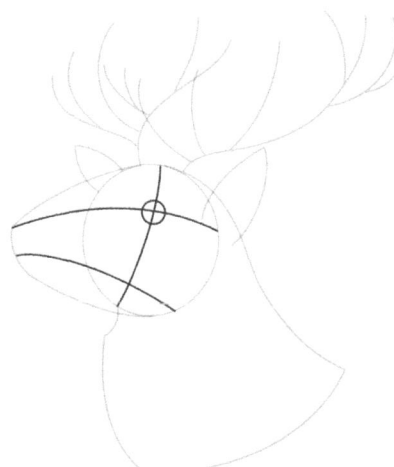

05

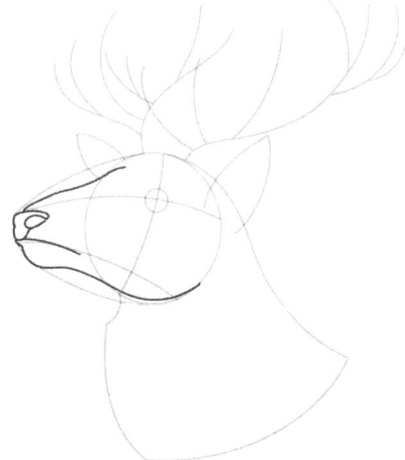

06

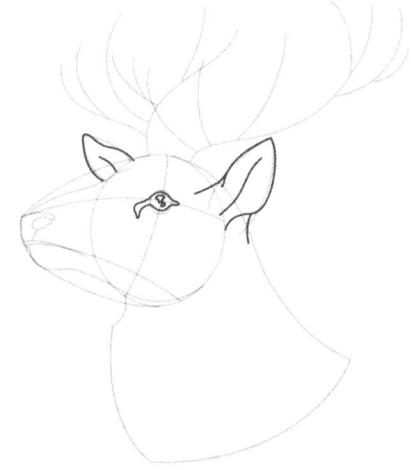

07

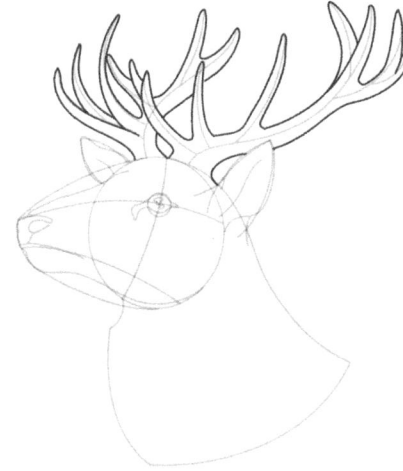

08

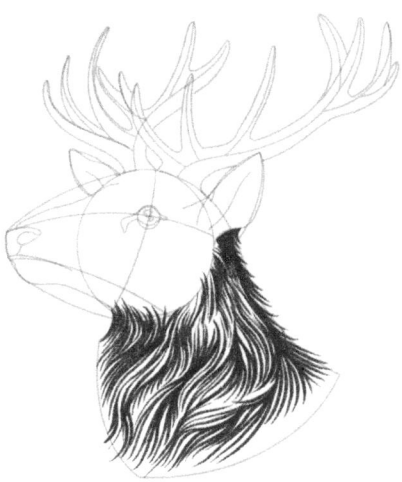

09

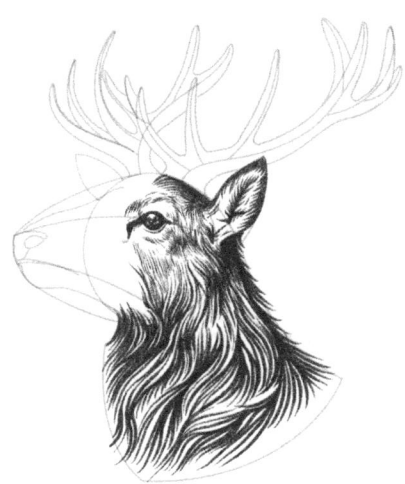

10

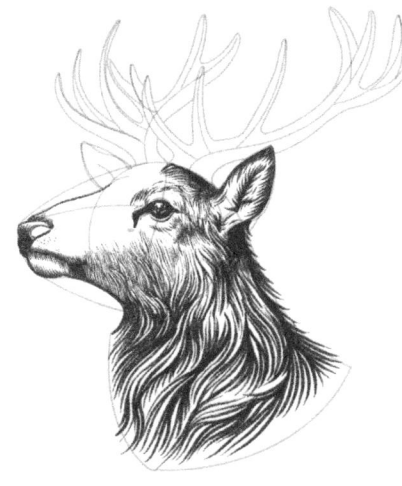

11

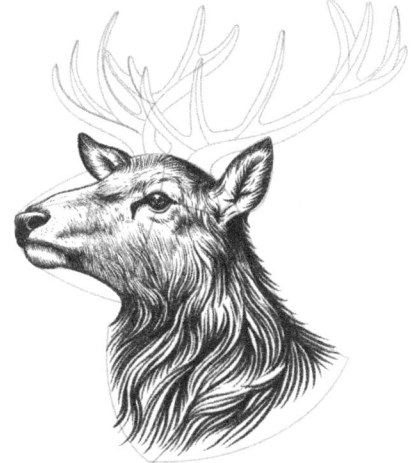

12

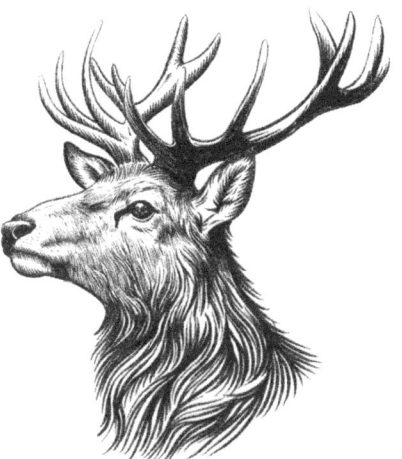

SWALLOW

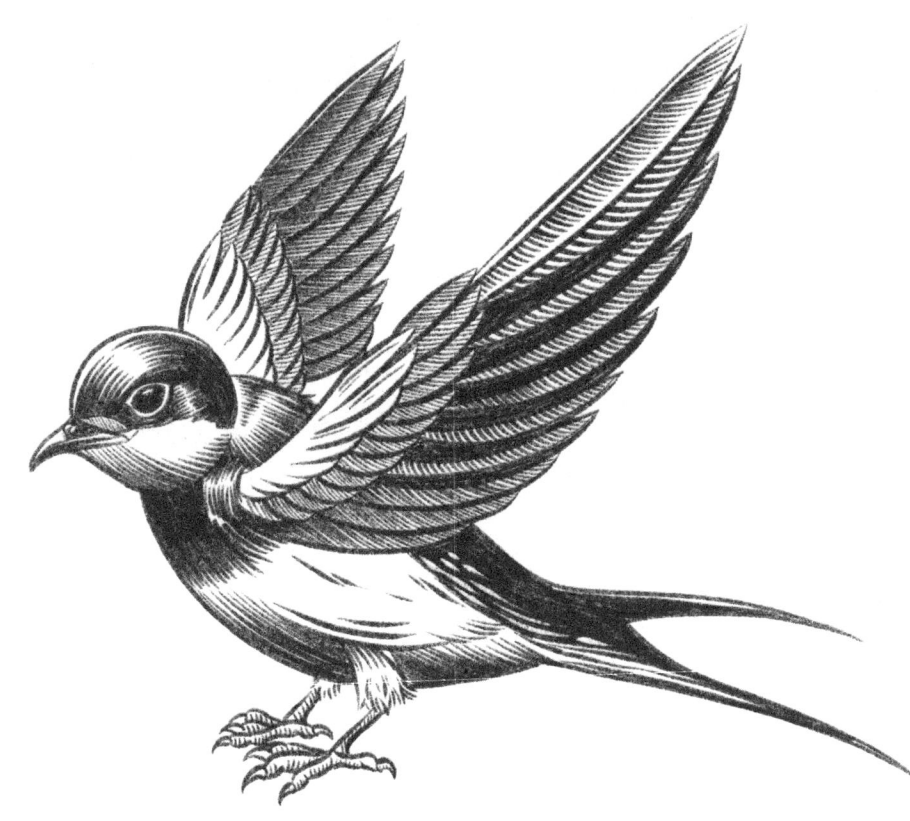

Pro Tip:
In step 04, when drawing the wings, ensure that the top point of the wing on the right side is slightly higher than on the left. Following this step will provide a natural-looking perspective.

01

02

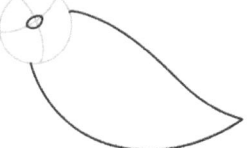

03

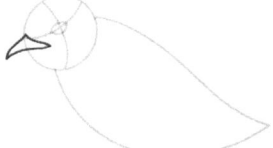

04

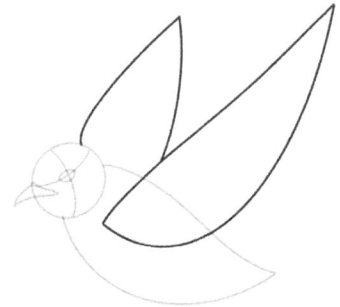

05

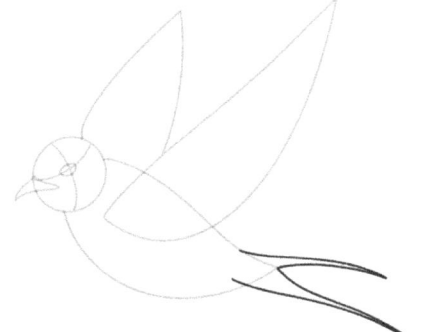

06

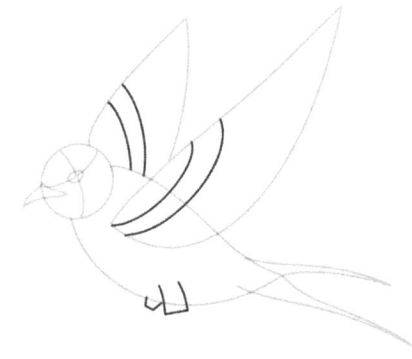

07

08

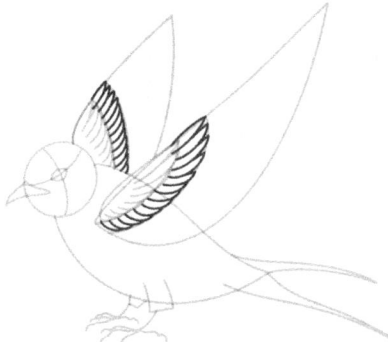

09

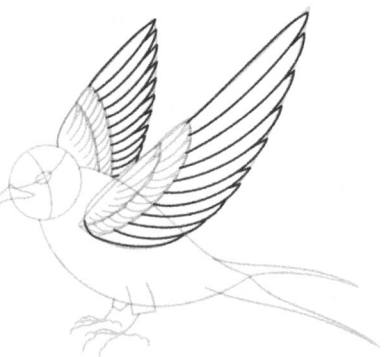

10

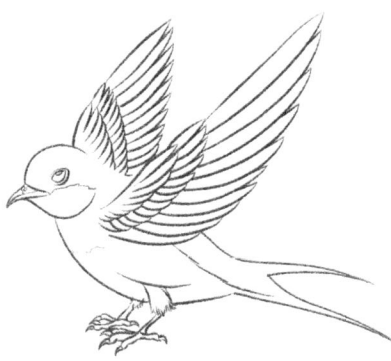

11

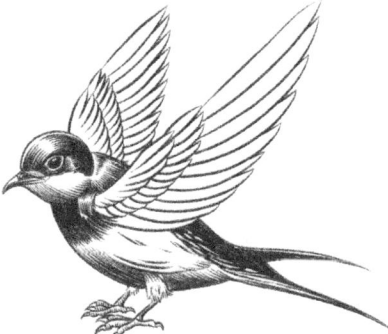

12

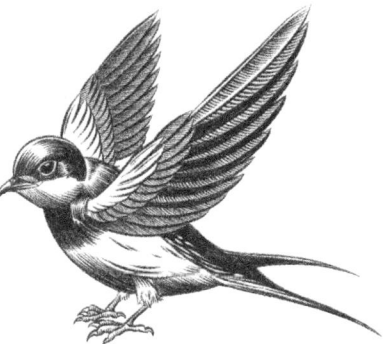

TIGER

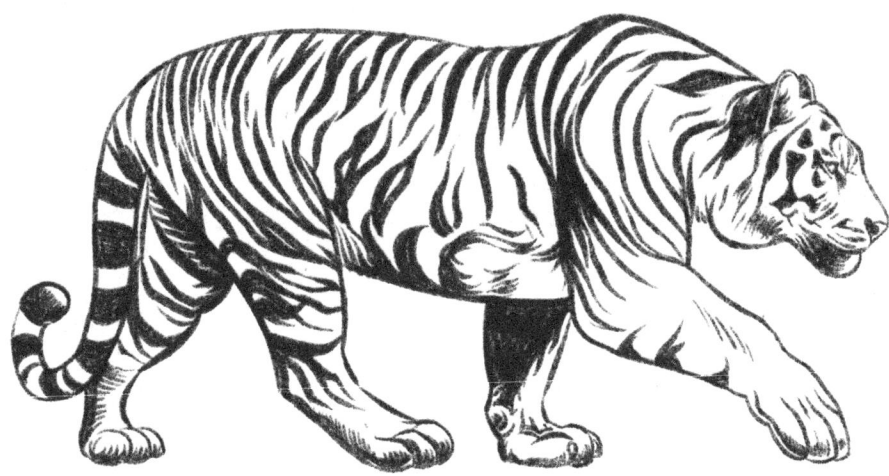

Pro Tip:
In step 01, the length of the line extending from the circle to the left is approximately four times the circle's width. Measure this distance from the outer left side of the circle.

01

02

03

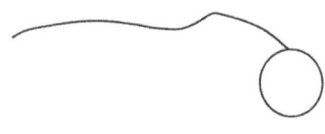

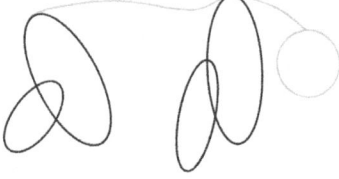

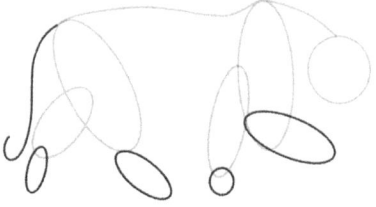

04

05

06

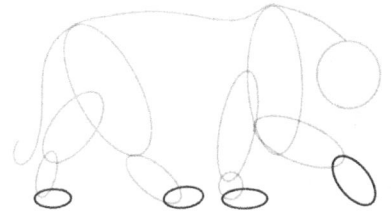
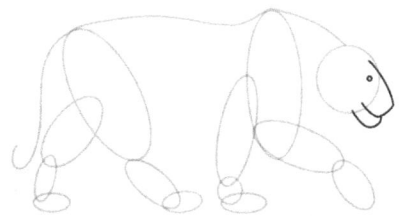
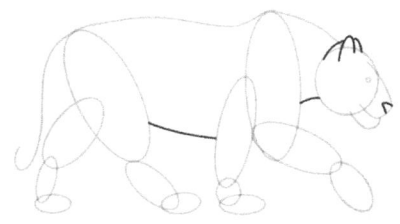

07

08

09

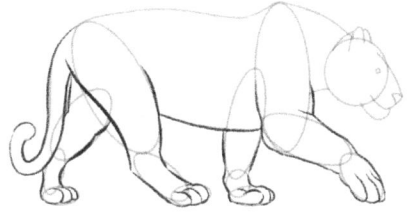
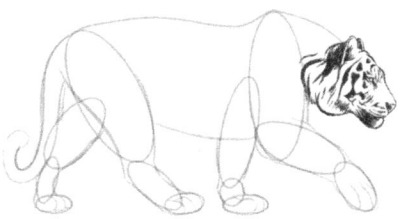
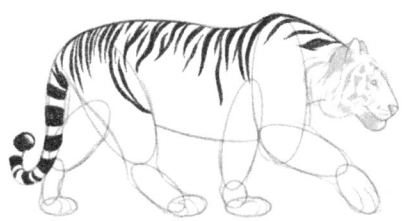

10

11

12

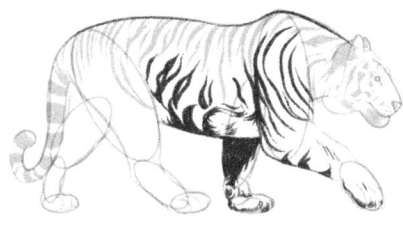
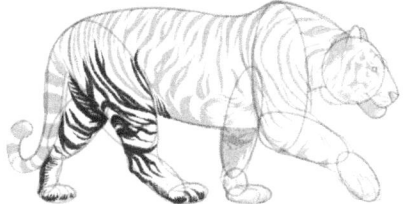
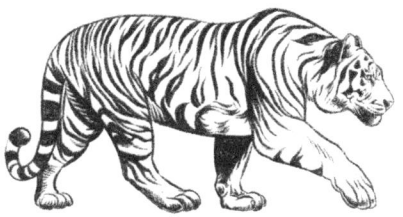

TIGER'S HEAD

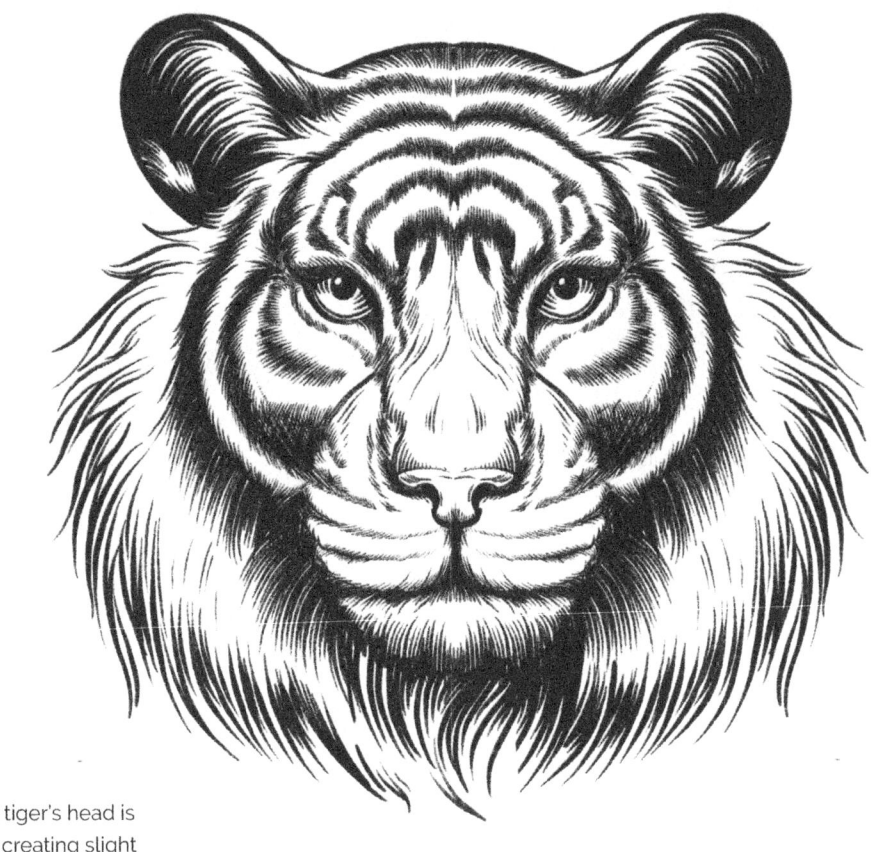

Pro Tip:
The design of the tiger's head is symmetrical, and creating slight variations in the line work and rendering between the left and right sides of the face provides a natural appearance.

01

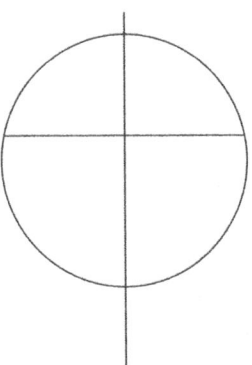

02

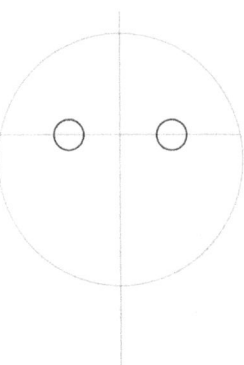

03

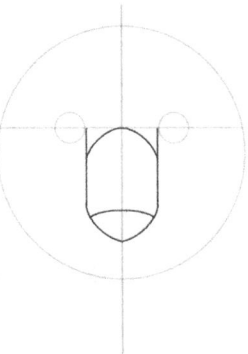

04

05

06

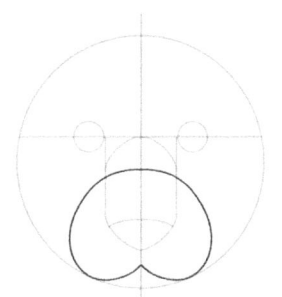
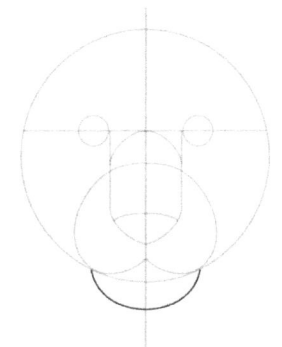
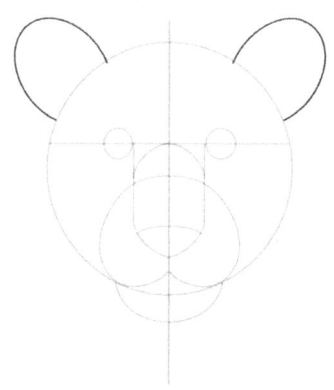

07

08

09

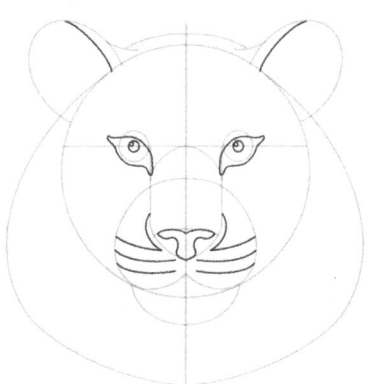
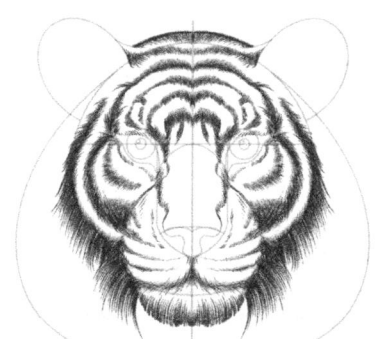

10

11

12

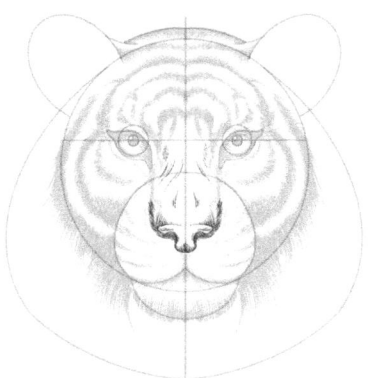
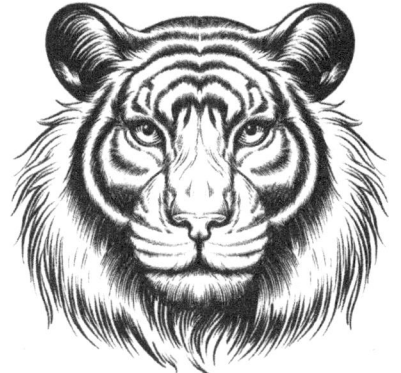

WALRUS

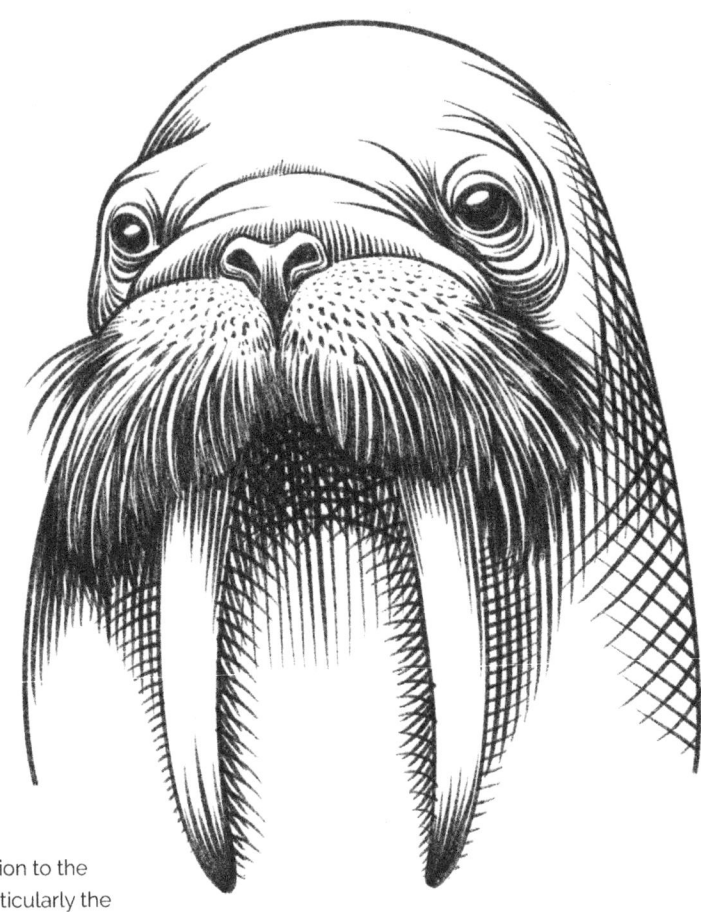

Pro Tip:
In step 02, pay close attention to the positioning of the eyes, particularly the one on the left. The eye must sit on the outer edge, almost touching it but not quite.

01

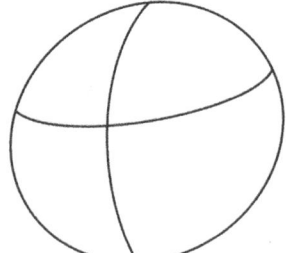

02

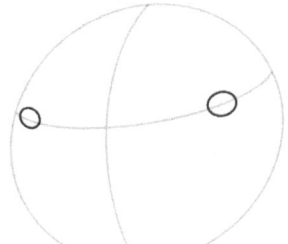

03

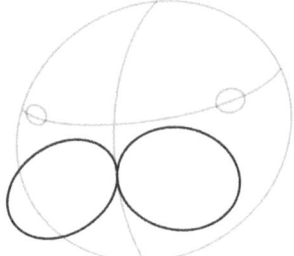

VOLUME.1 A STEP-BY-STEP GUIDE 76

04
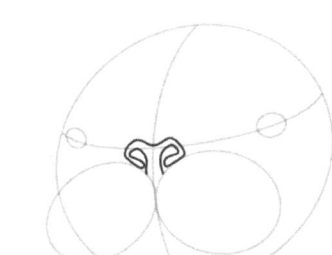

05
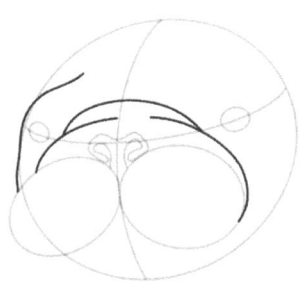

06
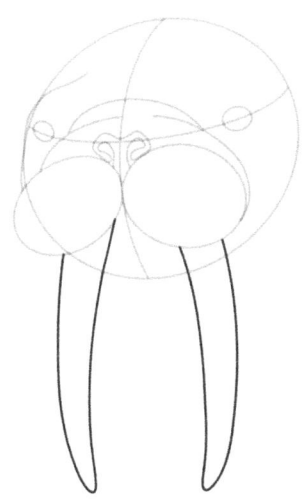

07
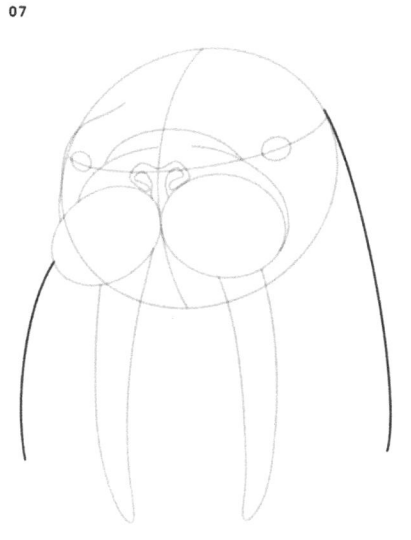

08
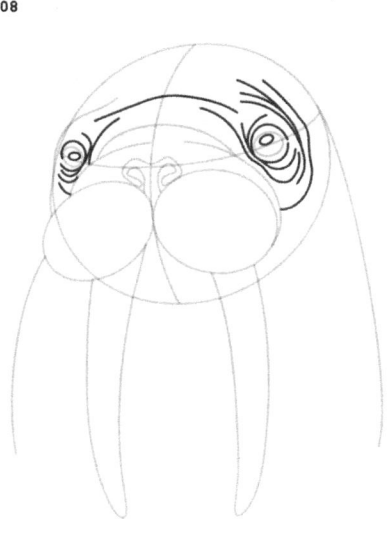

09
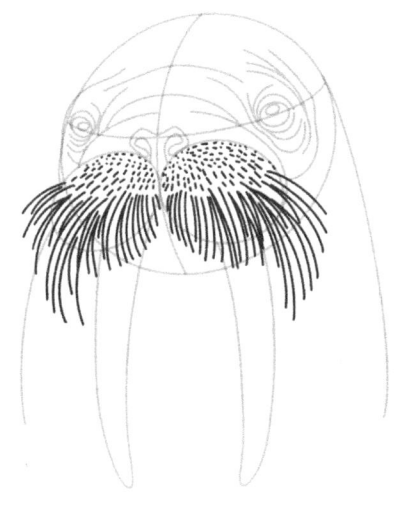

10
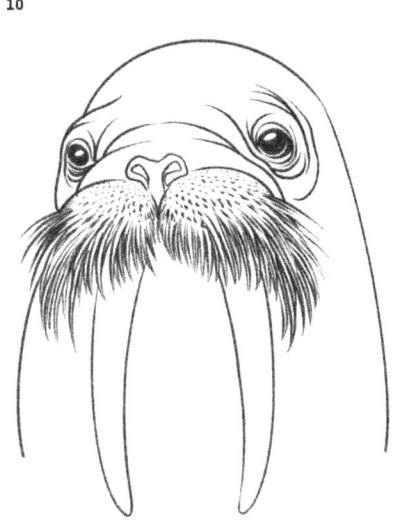

11
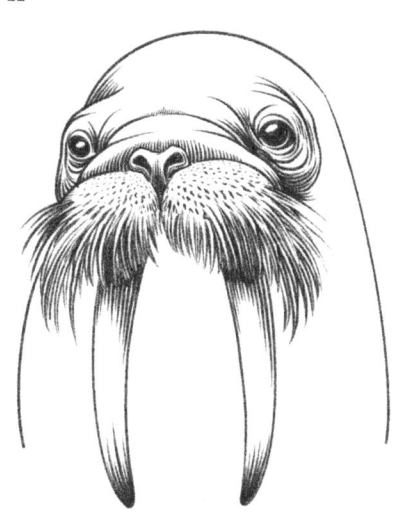

12
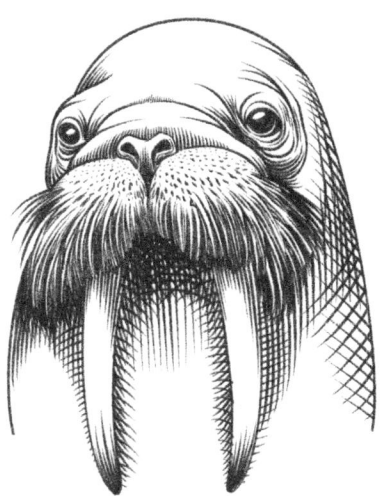

WHALE

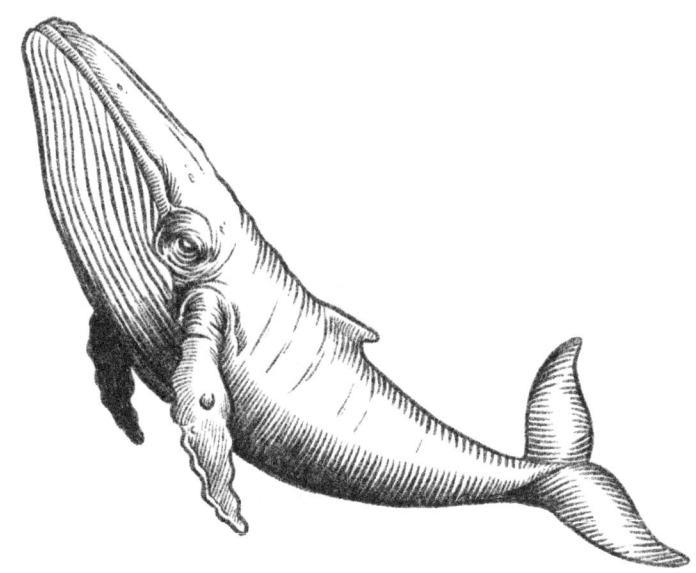

Pro Tip:
In step 02, when drawing the fins, ensure that the fin at the top is slightly smaller and set back to create the illusion of depth needed for a natural-looking perspective.

01

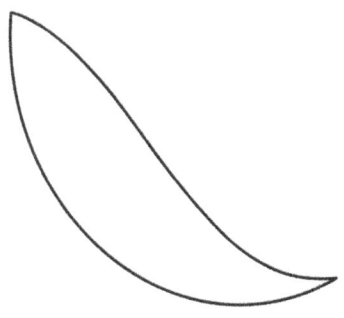

02

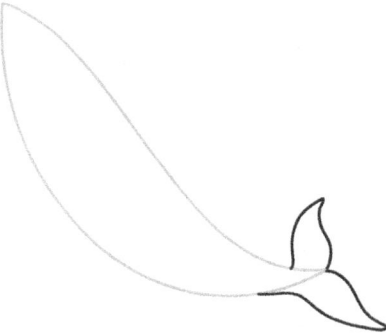

03

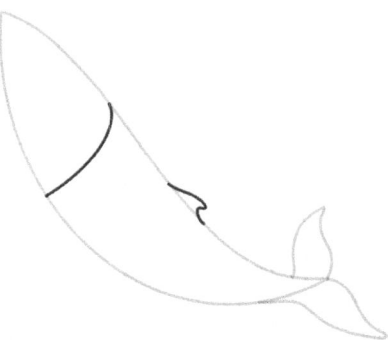

VOLUME.1 A STEP-BY-STEP GUIDE 78

04

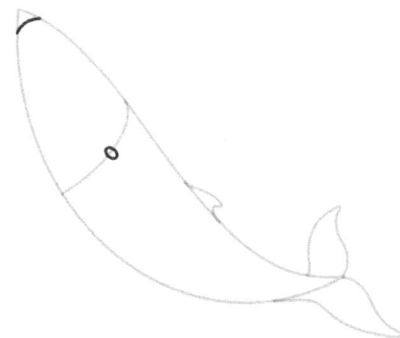

05

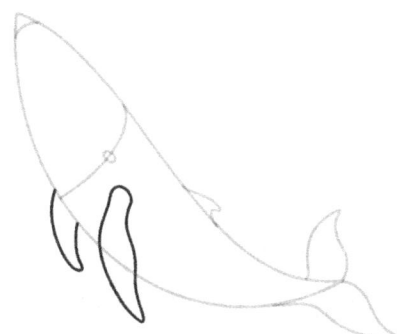

06

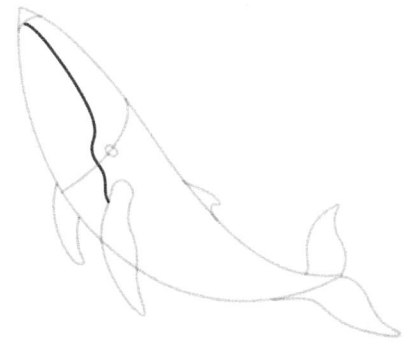

07

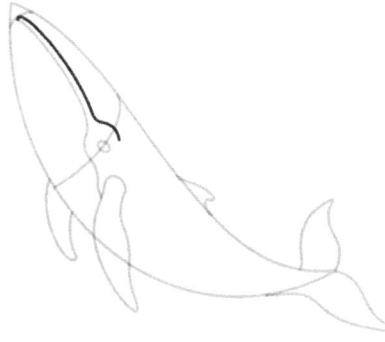

08

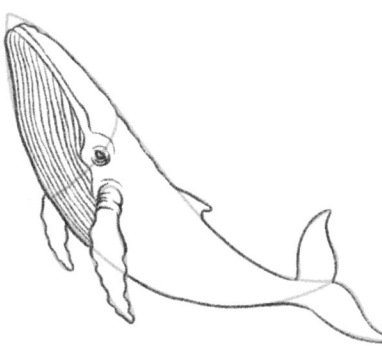

09

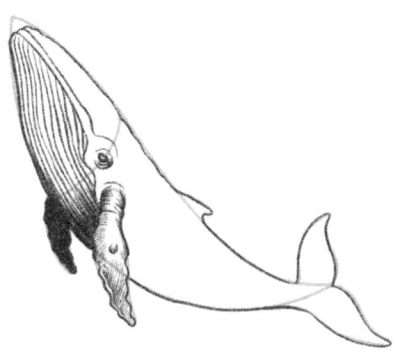

10

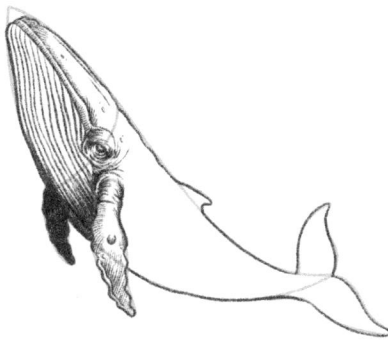

11

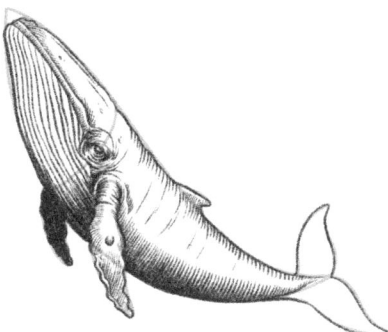

12

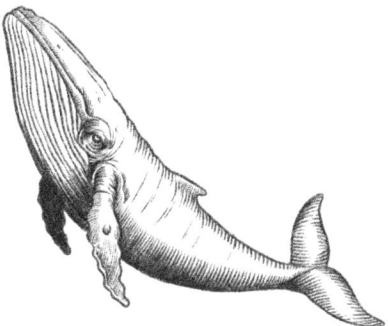

HOW TO DRAW ANIMALS

VAULTEDITIONS.COM

ZEBRA

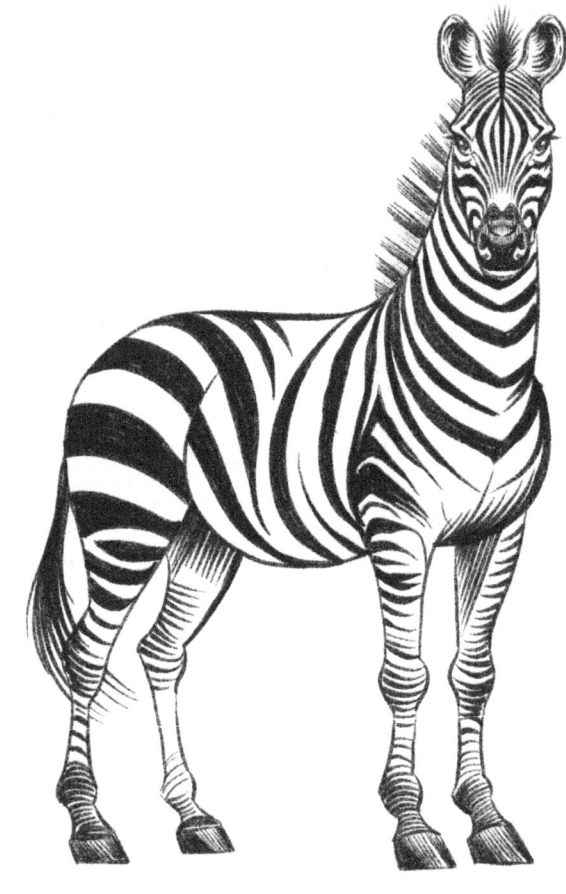

Pro Tip:
In step 12, use the guidelines and contours you have created to help inform the direction of the pattern of the zebra.

01

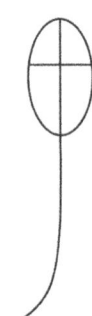

02

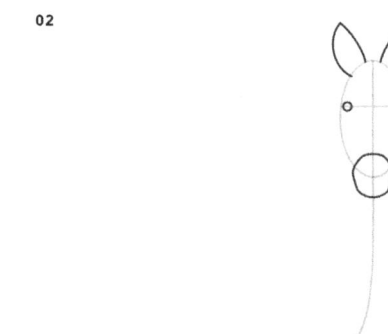

03

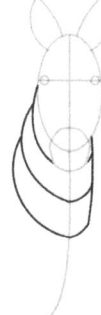

VOLUME.1 A STEP-BY-STEP GUIDE

04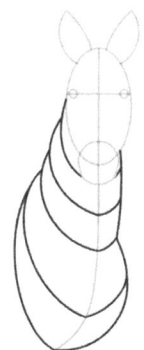
05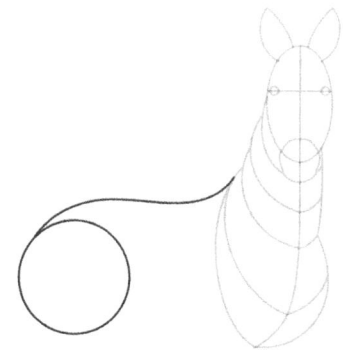
06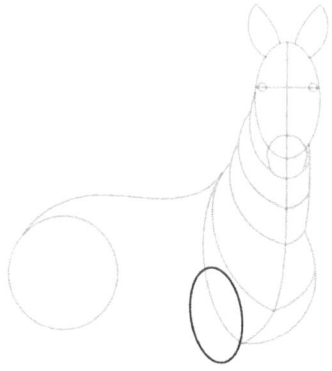

07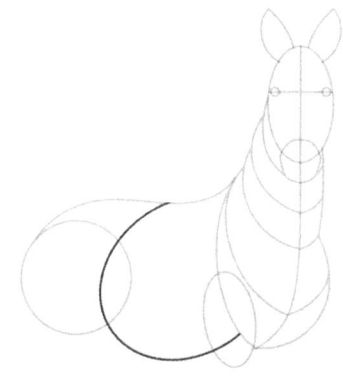
08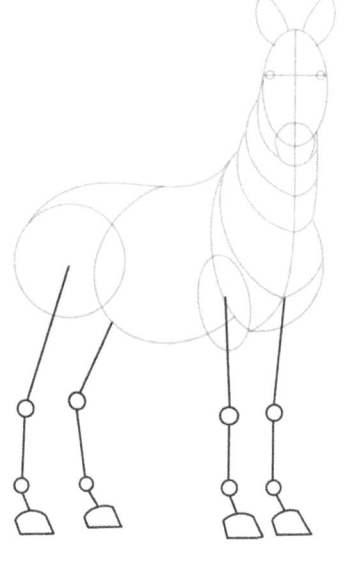
09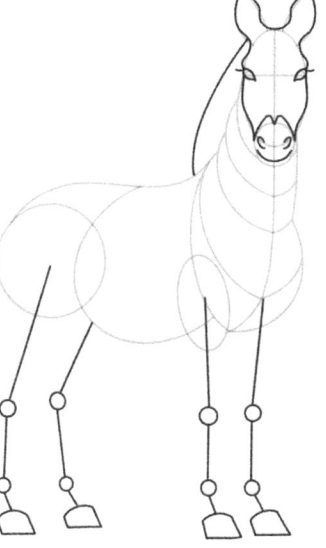

10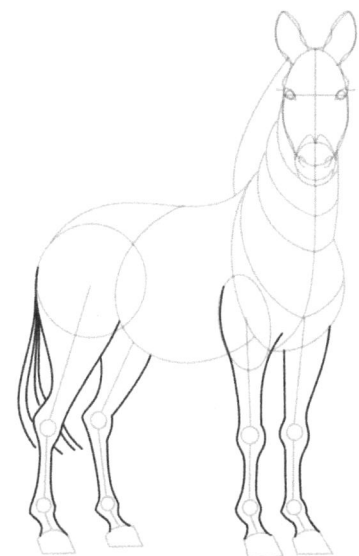
11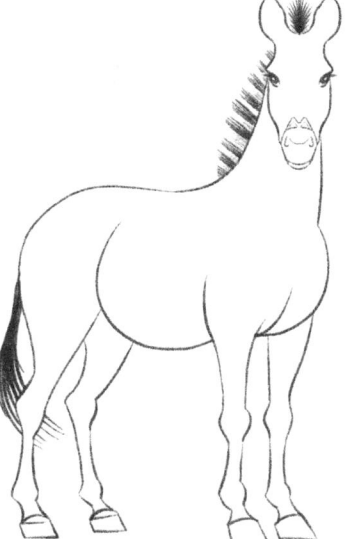
12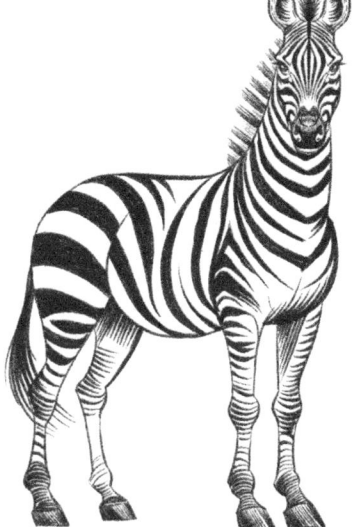

HOW TO DRAW ANIMALS

VAULTEDITIONS.COM

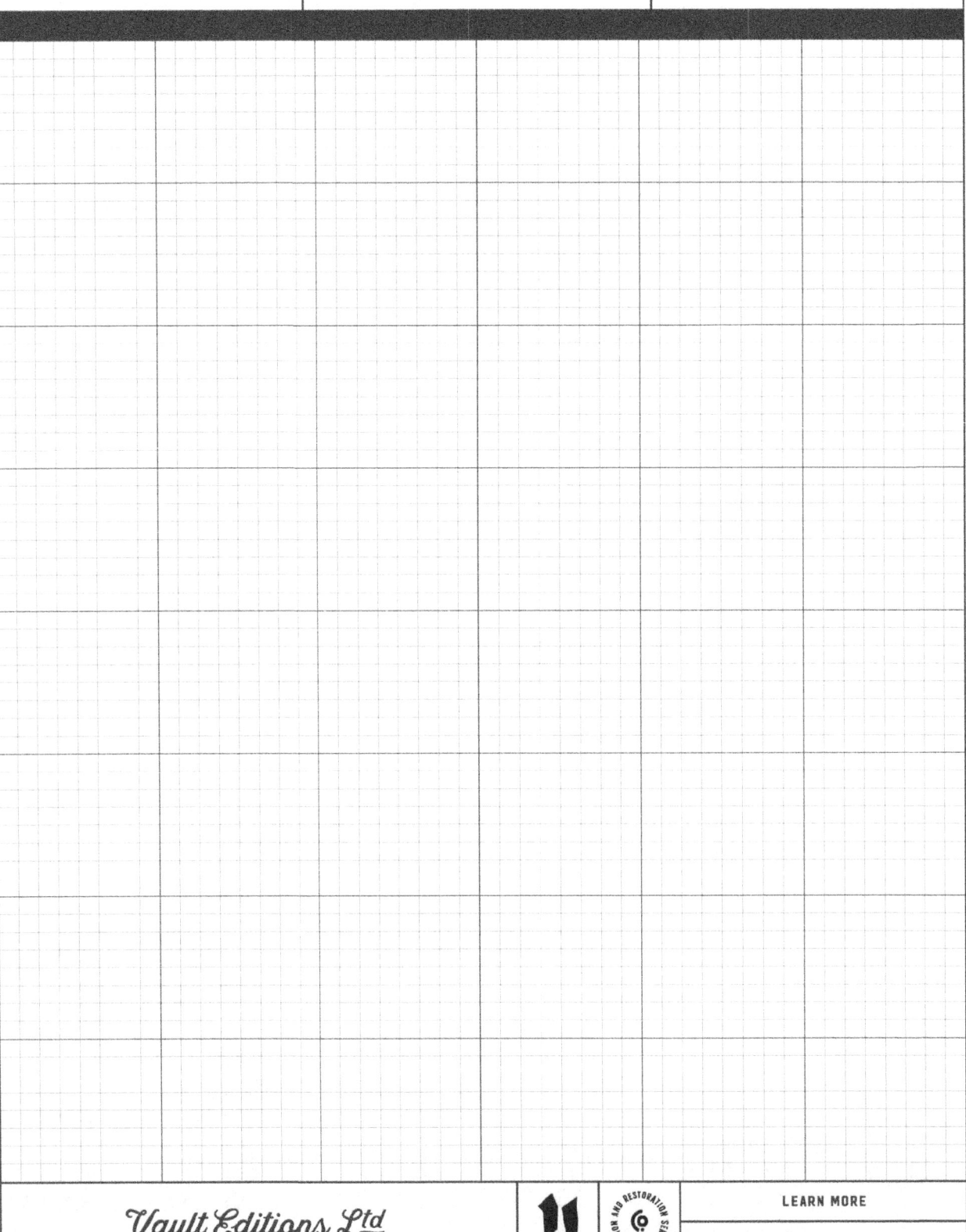

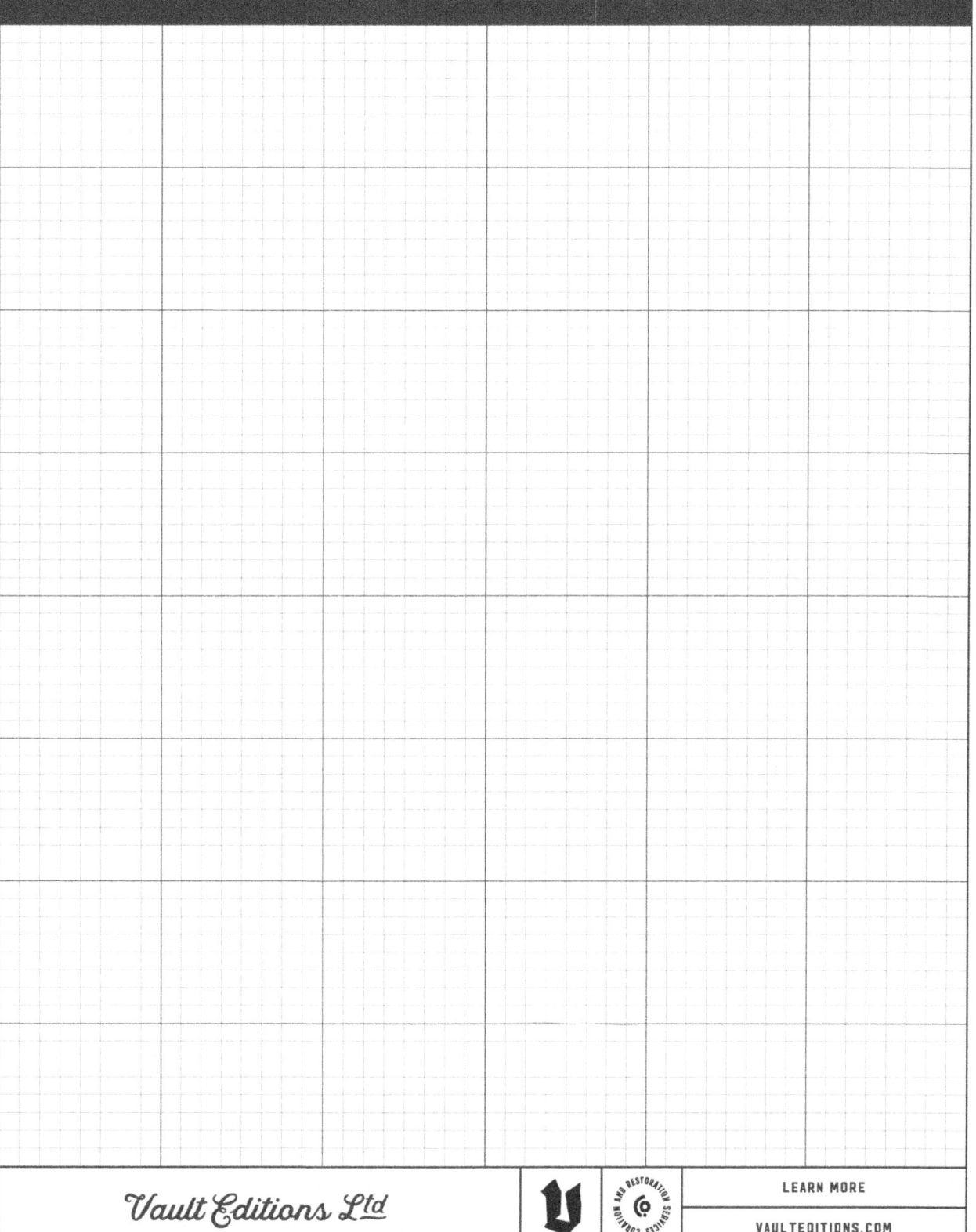

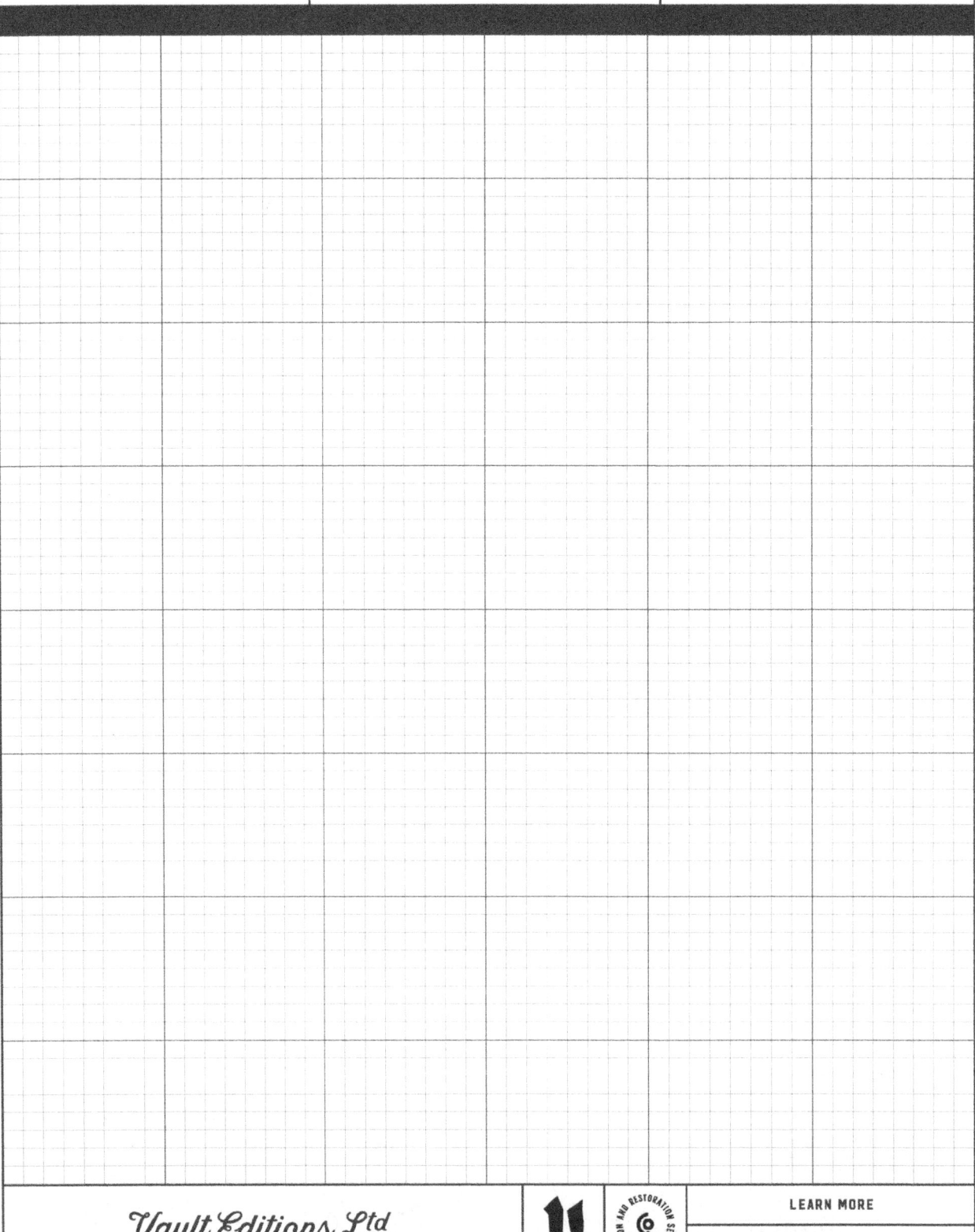

HOW TO DRAW ANIMALS

HOW TO DRAW ANIMALS

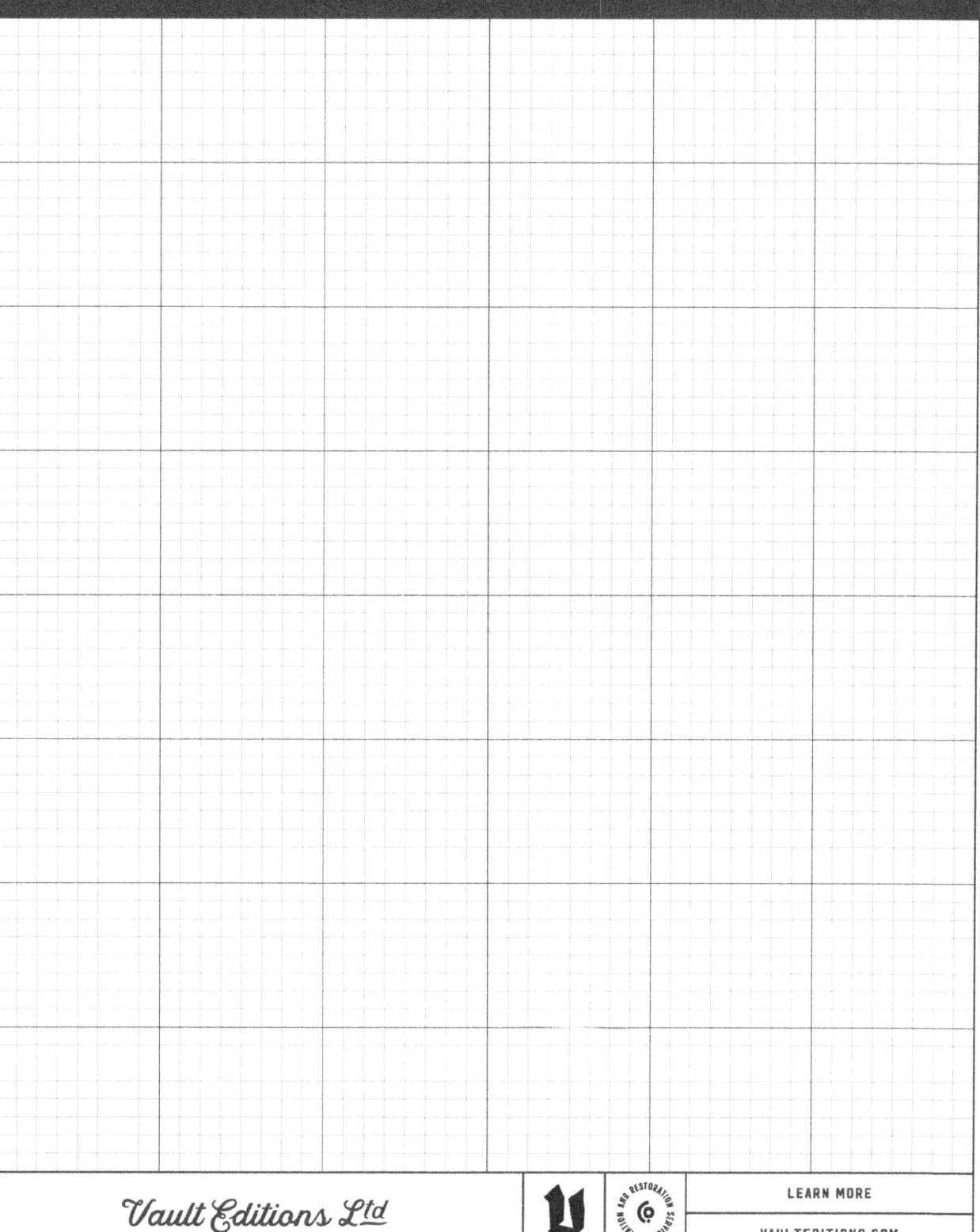

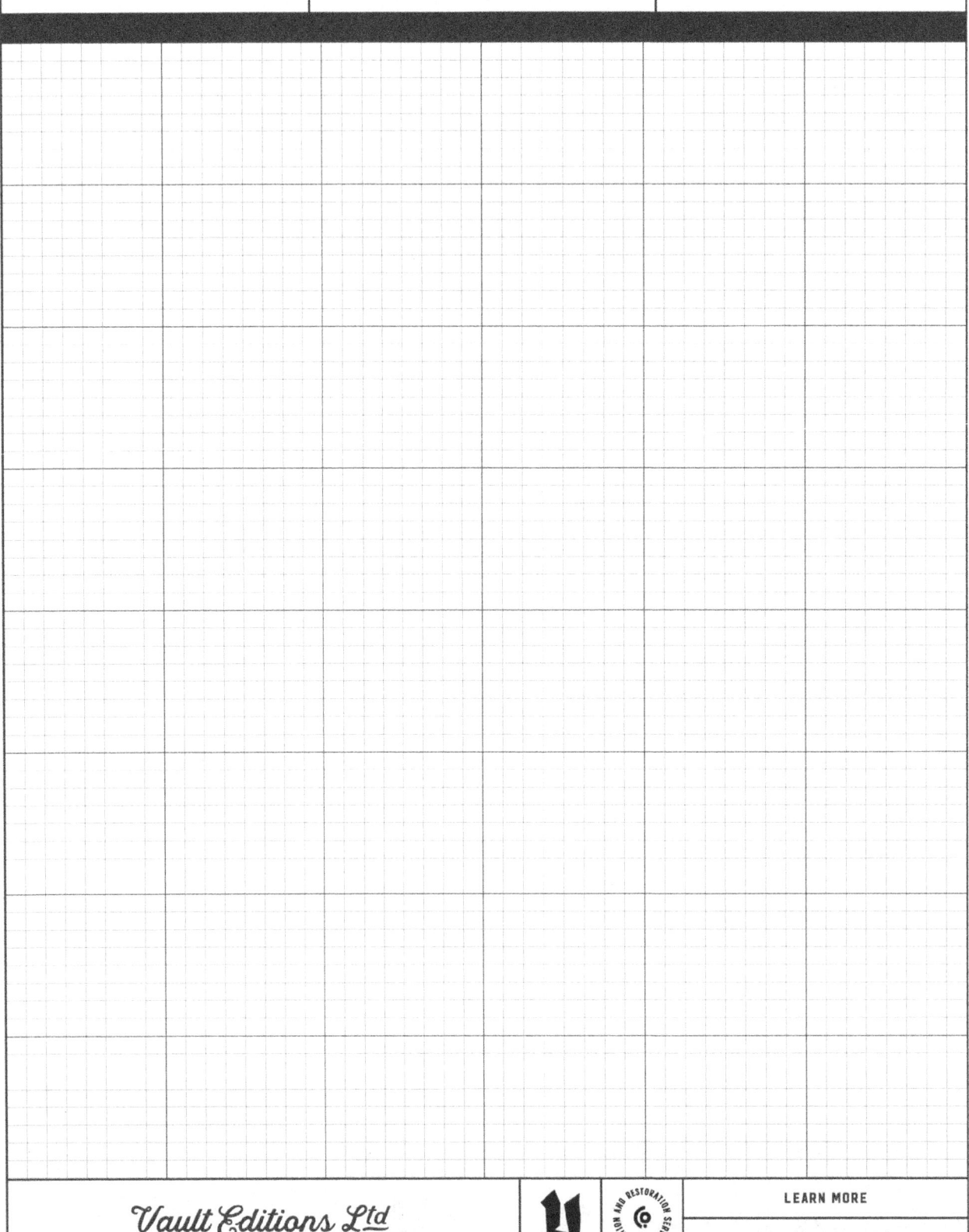

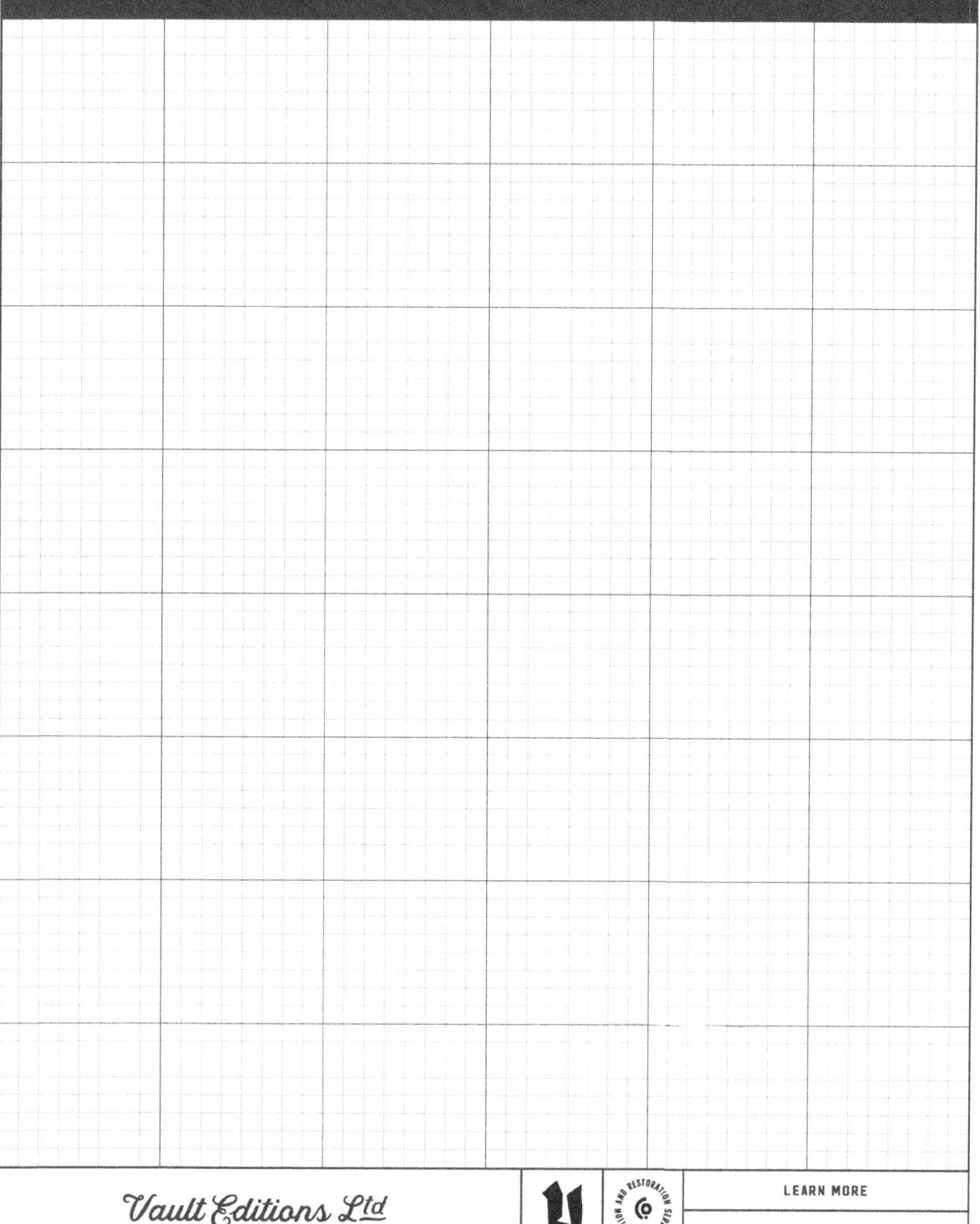

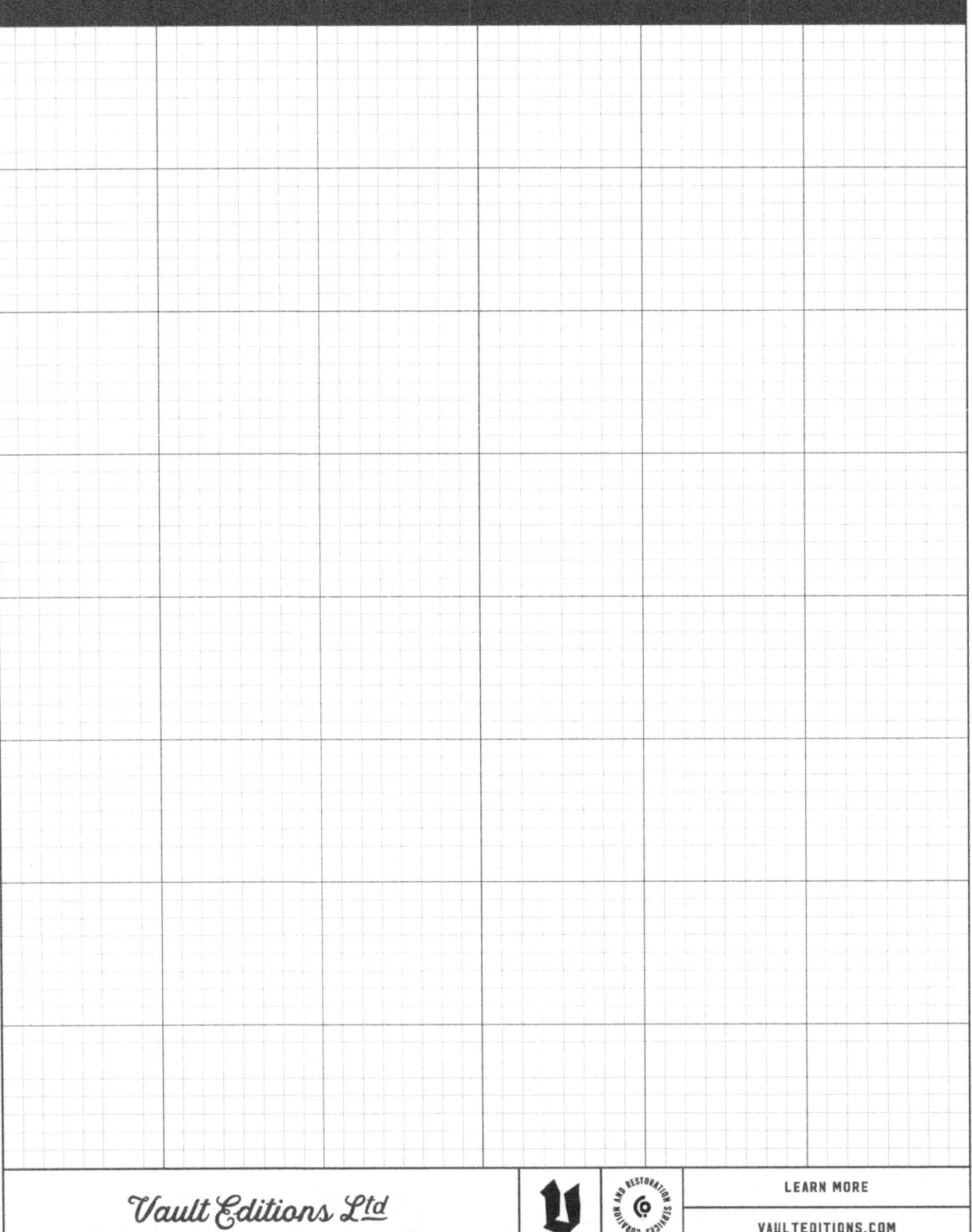

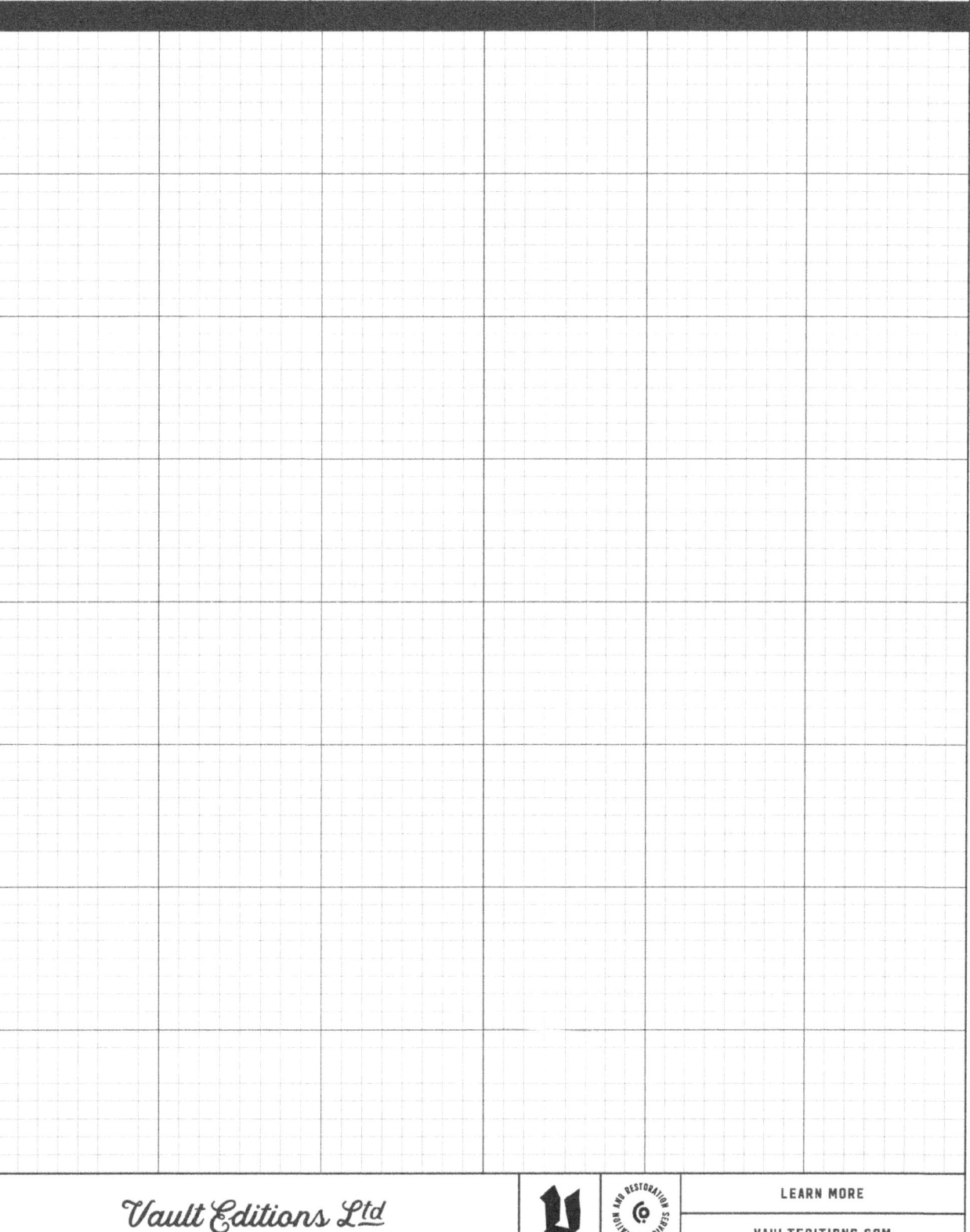

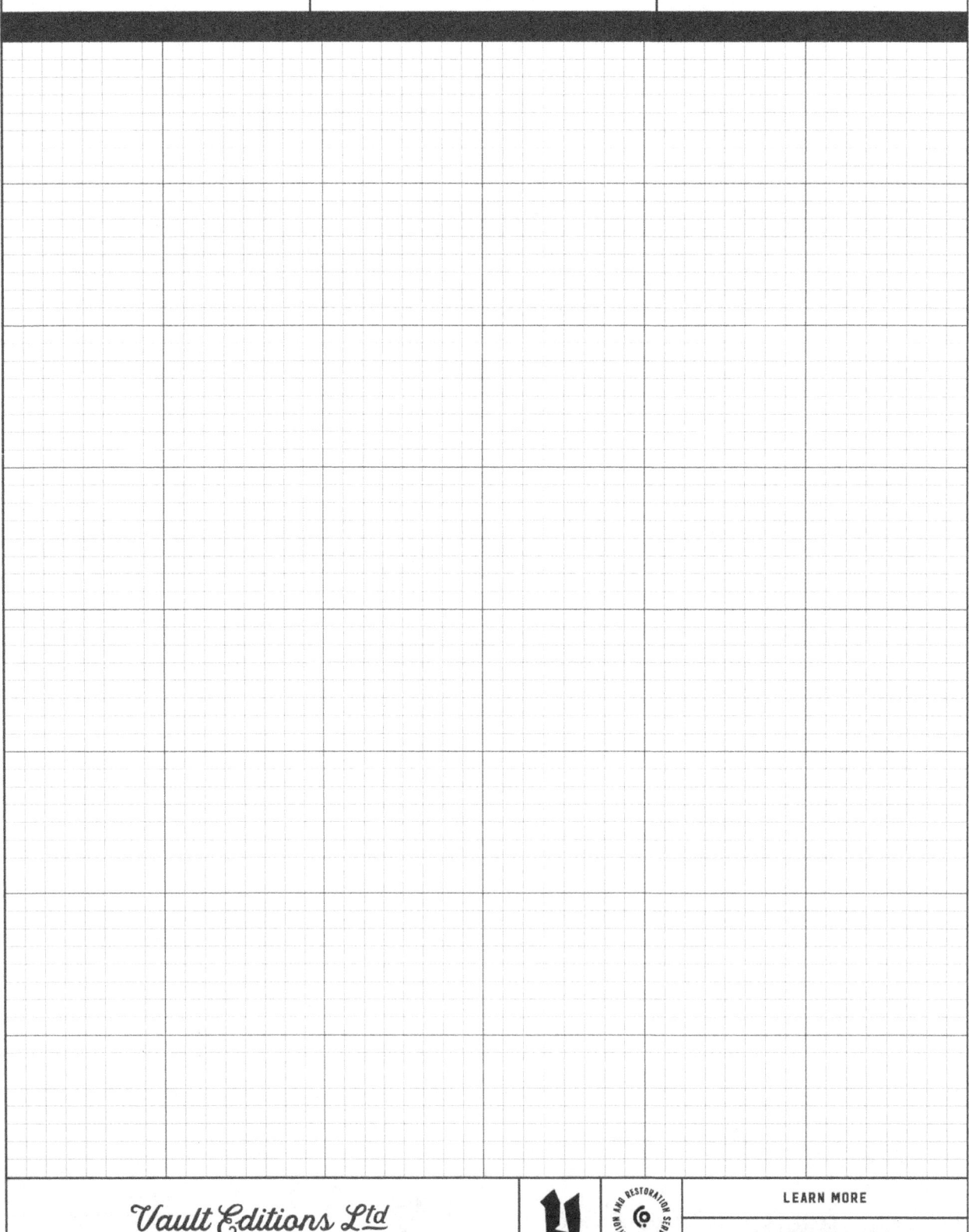

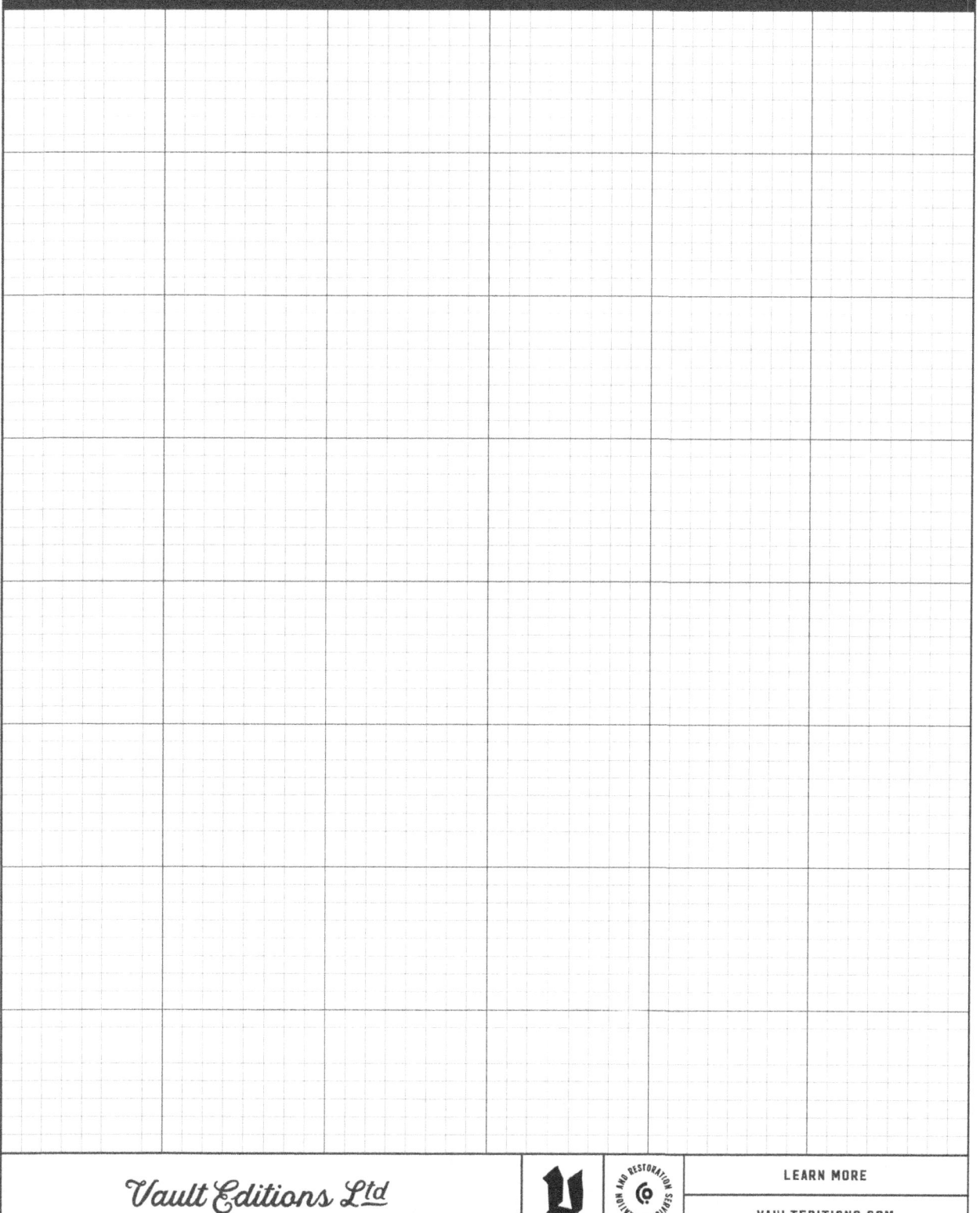

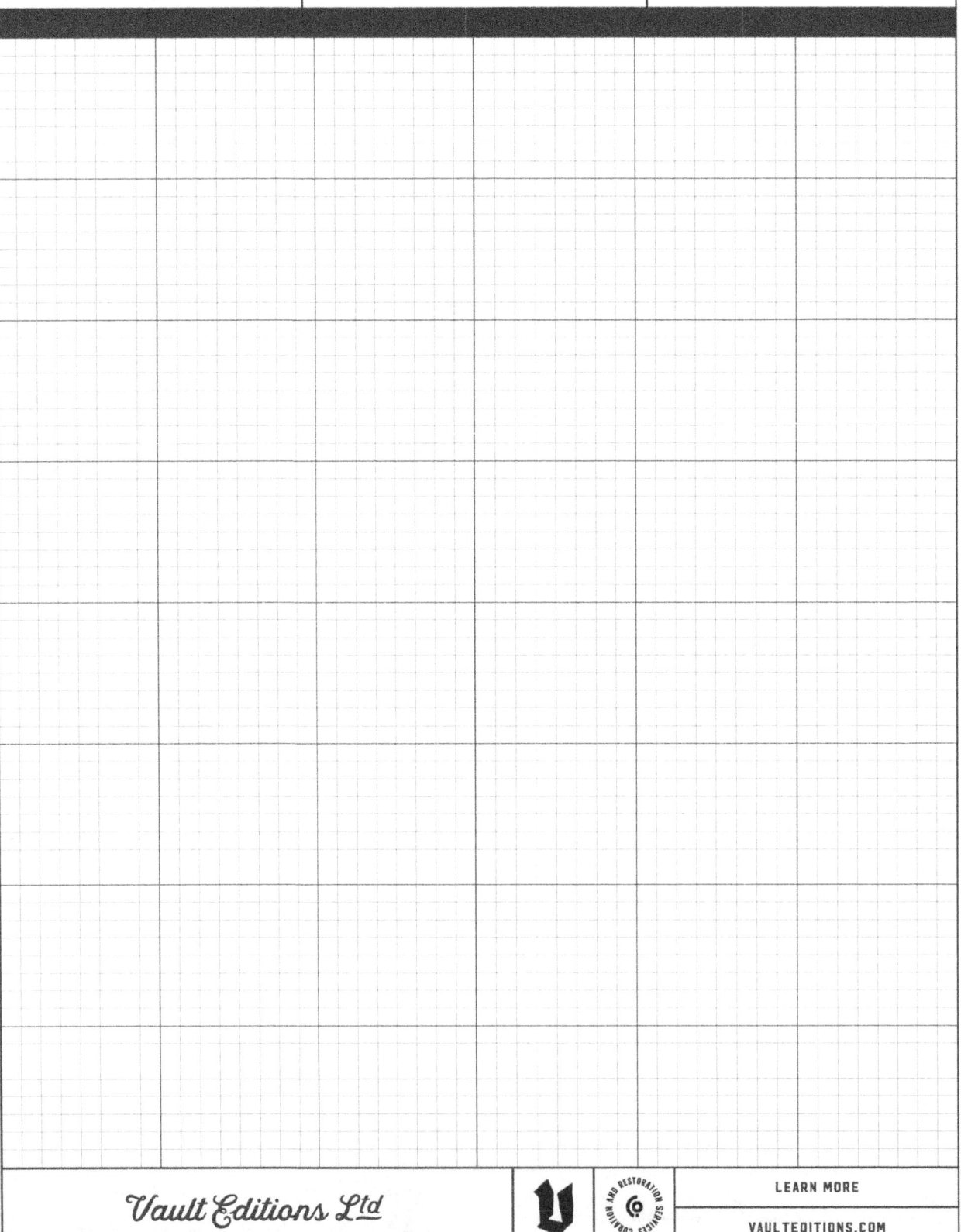

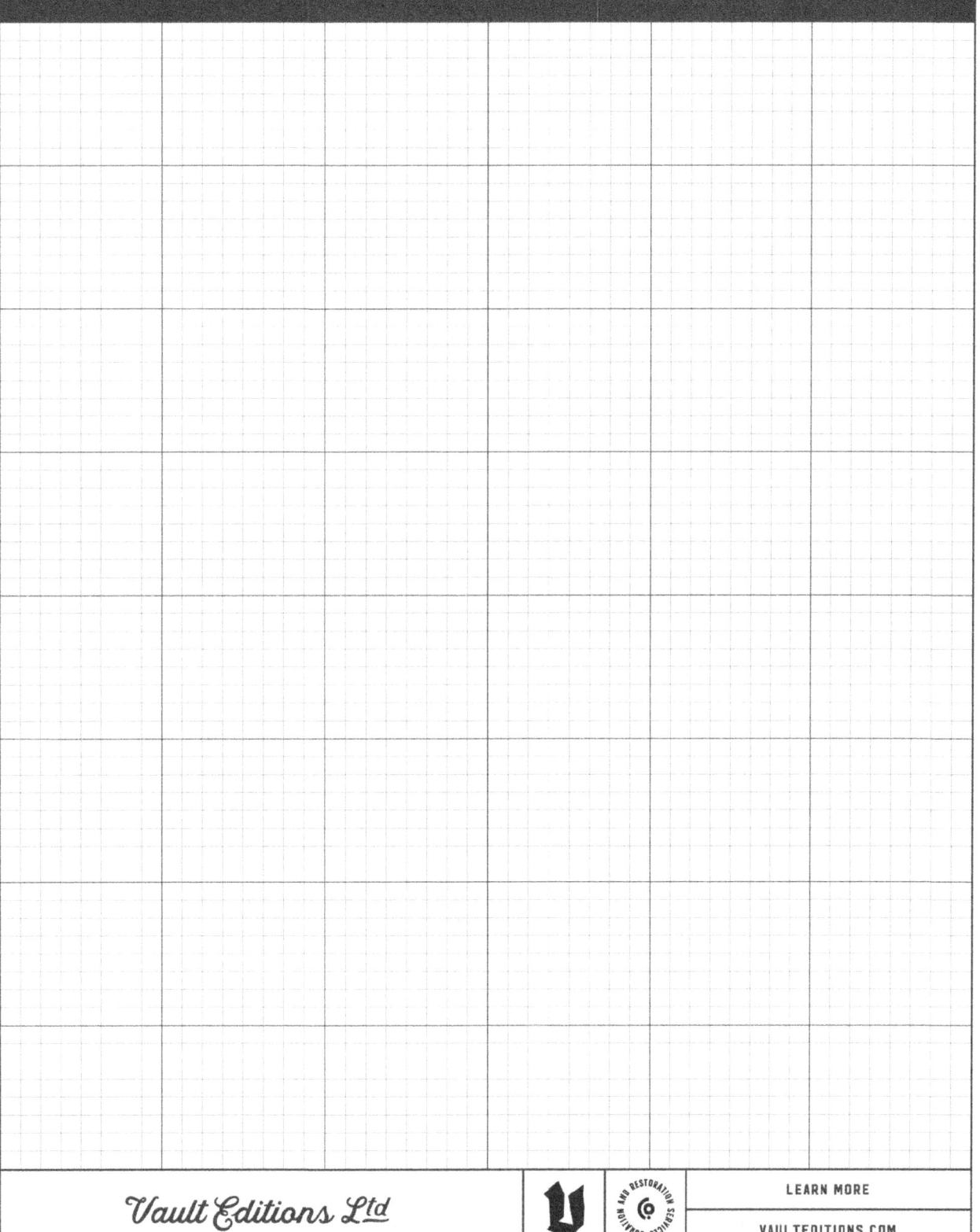

HOW TO DRAW ANIMALS

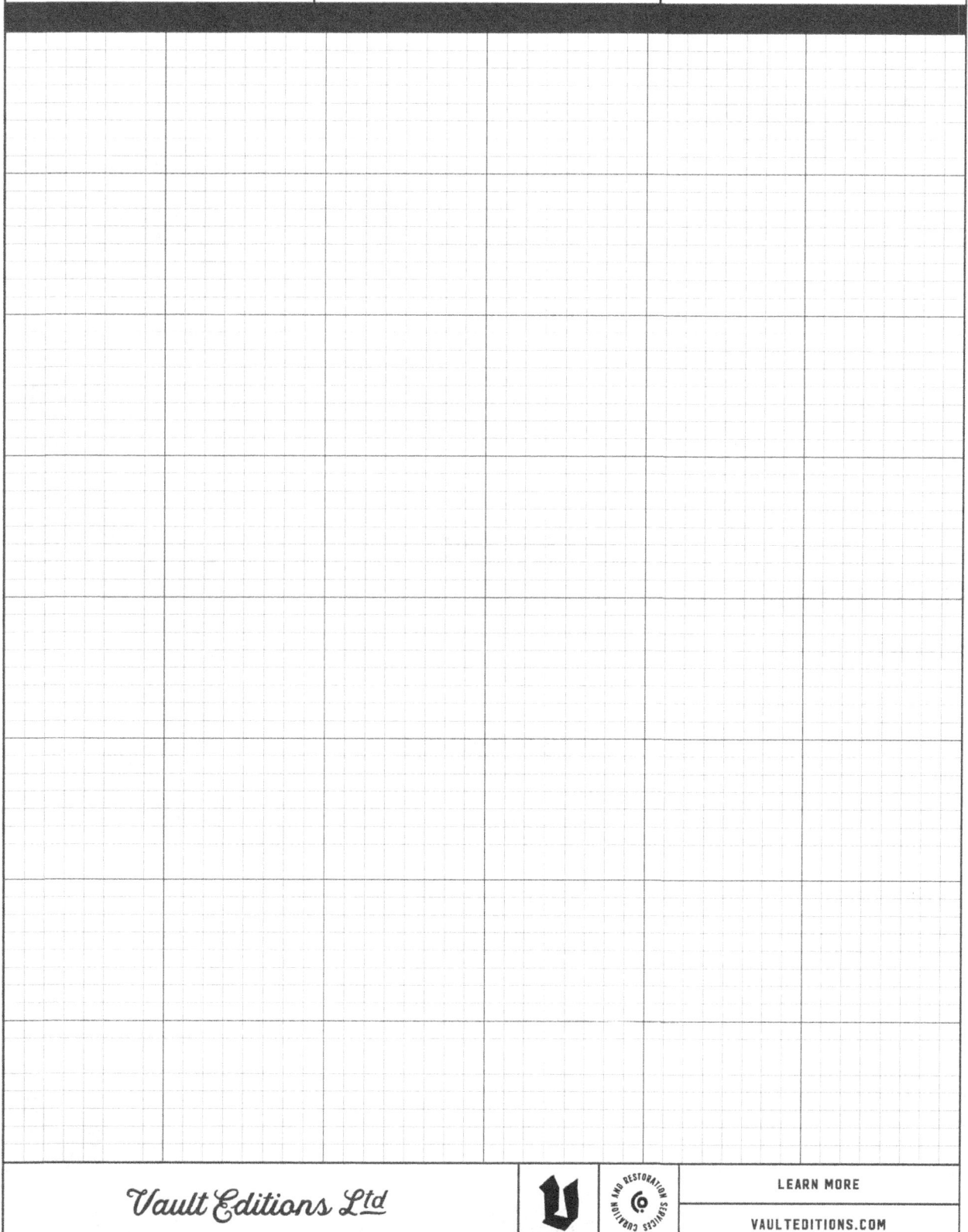

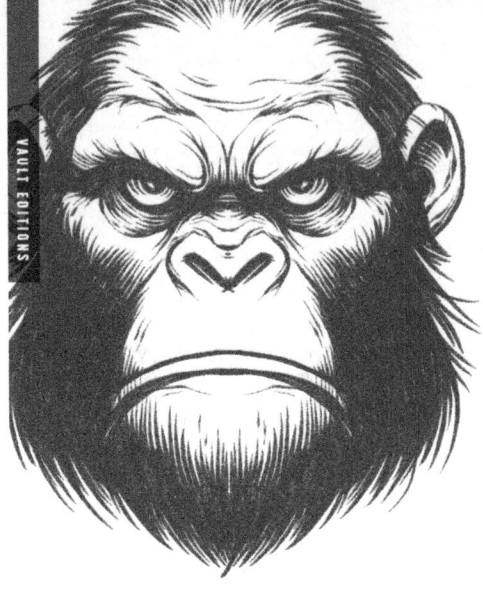

LEARN MORE

At Vault Editions, our mission is to create the world's most comprehensive collection of image archives for the practical use of artists and designers. If you have enjoyed this book, you can discover more of our titles at vaulteditions.com

REVIEW THIS BOOK

As a family-owned and operated independent publisher, reviews are essential to the success of our business. Please leave an honest review of this book wherever you purchased it.

JOIN OUR COMMUNITY

Are you the creative and curious type? If so, you will love our community on Instagram. We share bizarre and beautiful artwork ranging from 17th and 18th-century natural history and scientific illustrations to mythical beasts, ornamental designs, anatomical drawings and more; join our community of 280K+ people today by searching @vault_editions

VAULTEDITIONS.COM

STEP ONE

Enter the following web address on a desktop or laptop computer in your web browser.

vaulteditions.com/pages/htda

STEP TWO

Enter the following password to access the download page:

htda2735372sxda

STEP THREE

Follow the prompts to access your high-resolution files.

TECHNICAL SUPPORT

For technical support, please email: info@vaulteditions.com

Copyright © 2024
Vault Editions Ltd

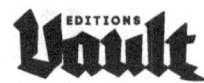

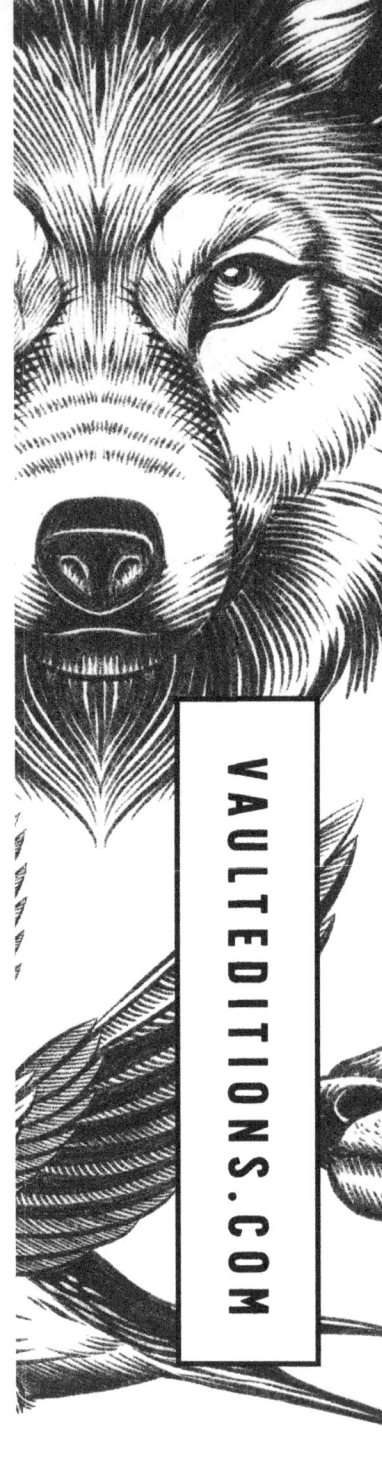

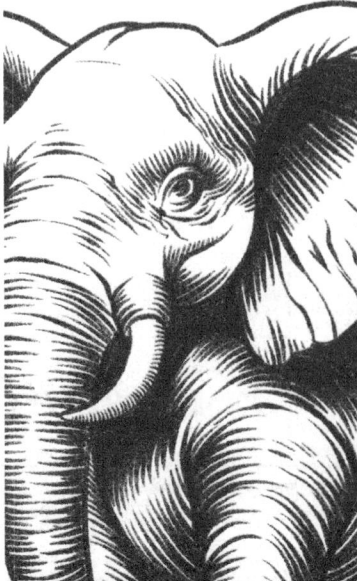

Made in United States
Orlando, FL
21 July 2024